READING - HENLEY-O

PANGBOURNE · SONNING COMMON · TWYF

C000257420

ROAD MAP   Page 2
READING ENLARGED CENTRE   Page 3
INDEX TO STREETS   Page 30

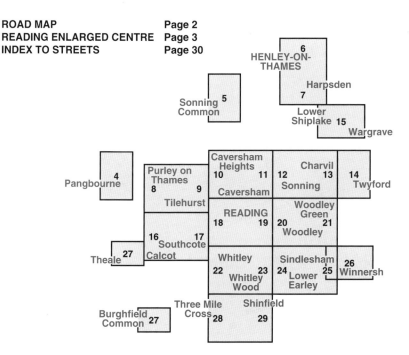

6
HENLEY-ON-THAMES

Harpsden
7

Sonning 5
Common

Lower
Shiplake 15

Wargrave

Pangbourne 4

Purley on
Thames
8   9

Tilehurst

Caversham
Heights
10   11

Caversham

Charvil
12   13

Sonning

14
Twyford

READING
18   19

Woodley
Green
20   21

Woodley

16   17
Southcote

Theale 27 Calcot

Whitley
22   23
Whitley
Wood

Sindlesham
24   25

Lower
Earley

26
Winnersh

Three Mile
Cross

Shinfield

Burghfield 27
Common

28   29

Every effort has been made to verify
the accuracy of information in this
book but the publishers cannot accept
responsibility for expense or loss
caused by an error or omission.
Information that will be of assistance
to the user of the maps will be welcomed.

The representation on these maps of a
road, track or path is no evidence of the
existence of a right of way.

Car Park	P
Public Convenience	C
Place of Worship	+
One-way Street	→
Pedestrianized	▨
Post Office	●

**Scale of street plans 4 inches to 1 mile
Unless otherwise stated**

Street plans prepared and published by ESTATE PUBLICATIONS, Bridewell House,
TENTERDEN, KENT, and based upon the ORDNANCE SURVEY mapping with the permission
of The Controller of H. M. Stationery Office.

The Publishers acknowledge the co-operation of the local authorities
of towns represented in this atlas.

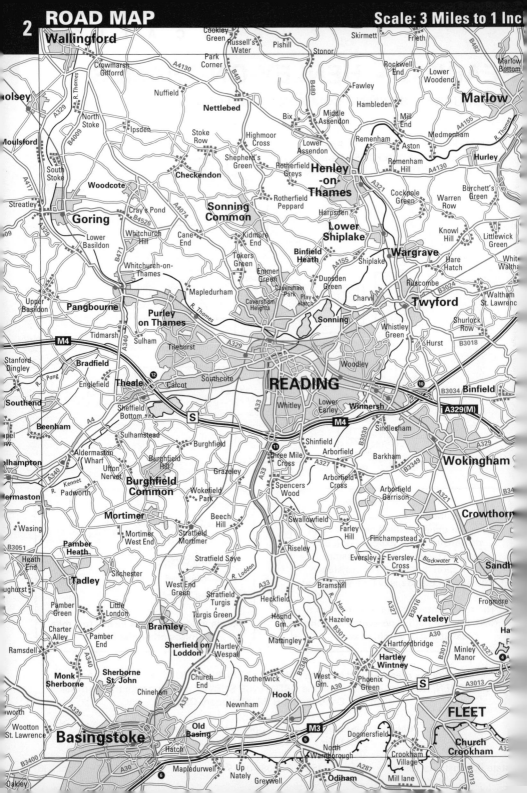

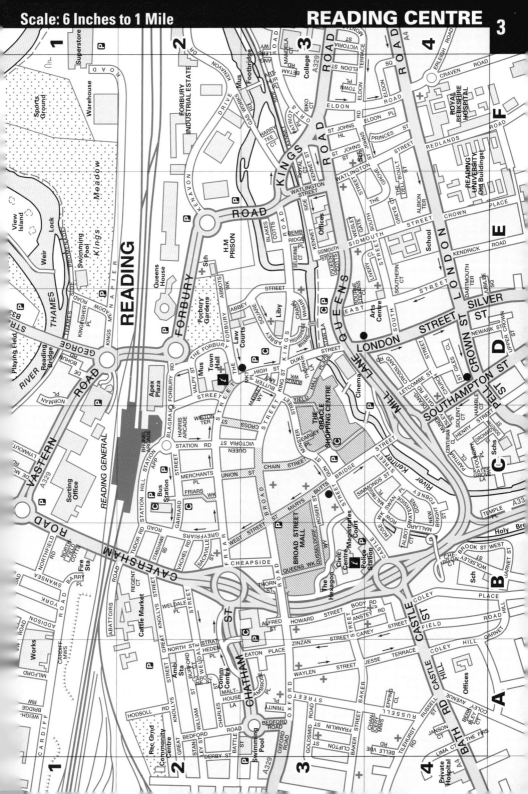

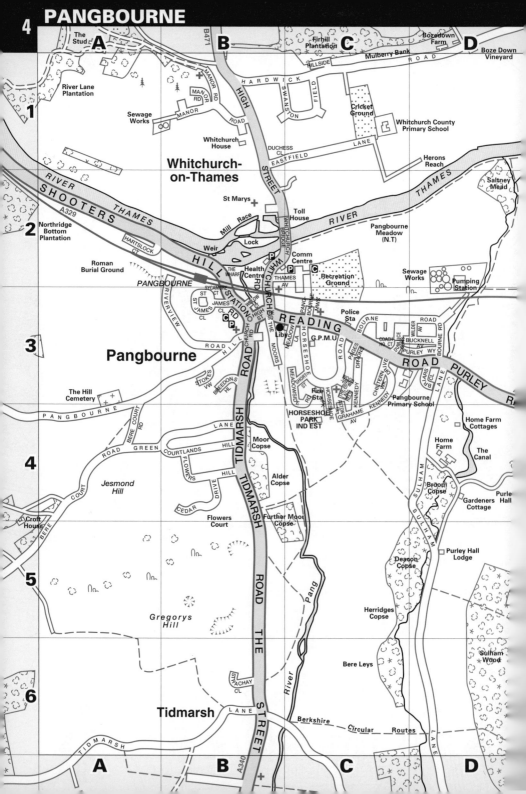

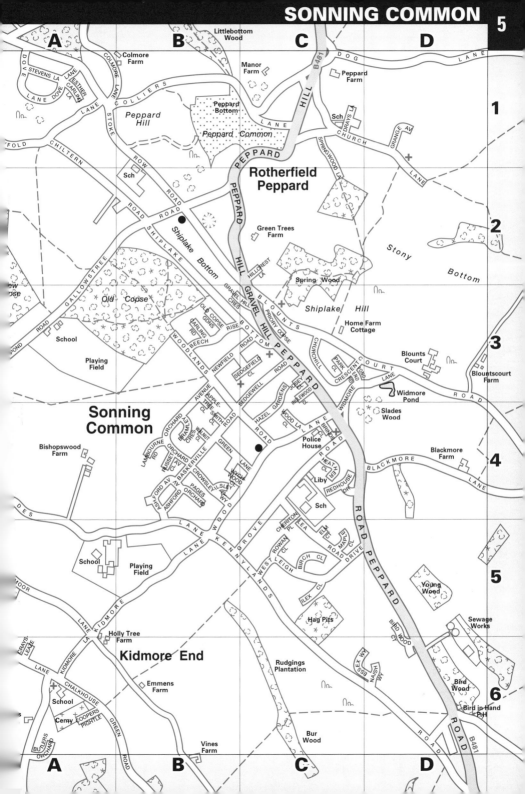

A **B** **C** **D**

Littlebottom
Wood

Colmore
Farm

DOVE
LANE

STEVENS LA

ESTHER

CARLIN

DOVE LA

COLMORE
LANE

STOKE
ROW
ROAD

CHILTERN

FOLD

COLLIERS
LANE

Peppard
Hill

Peppard
Bottom

Peppard Common

Manor
Farm

Peppard
Farm

DOG   LANE

B481

HILL

CHURCH   LANE

SPRINGWOOD LA

Sch

DRAYS LA

GRANGE AV

LANE

1

**Rotherfield
Peppard**

Sch

ROW

ROAD

PEPPARD

PEPPARD
HILL

Green Trees
Farm

GRAVEL HILL

HILLCREST LA

Spring Wood

Stony

Bottom

2

Shiplake Bottom

Old Copse

GALLOWSTREE
ROAD

WOODLANDS

OLD COPSE
CRES

RISE

DARLING
GDNS

BEECH

NEWFIELD
ROAD

GRAVEL HILL BOTTOM

PEPPARD

B PRIORY COPSE

BLOUNTS

Shiplake Hill

Home Farm
Cottage

CHURCHILL

PARK
CL

CRESCENT

COURT

Blounts
Court

Blountscourt
Farm

3

School

Playing
Field

POND

AVENUE

SEDGEFIELD
CL

APPLE
TREE
SMITH ROAD

SEDGEWELL

ROAD

CL

HAZEL GARDENS

INGLEWOOD

WOOD LA LANE

WIDMORE

LANE

ROAD

Widmore
Pond

Slades
Wood

**Sonning
Common**

Bishopswood
Farm

LAMBOURNE
RD

ORCHARD

RUSSELL
CL

ORCHARD

BRAMBLE
CL

WALNUT
CRES

BASKERVILLE ROAD

GREEN

CROWSLEY

PAGES
ORCHARD

LANE

WYCH
WOOD

SEDGEWELL
ROAD

HEATH

BRINDS

SPRINGS

ROAD

Police
House

HEATHER
DR

REDHOUSE

Blackmore
Farm

BLACKMORE   LANE

4

ASHFORD AV

FORD ROAD

LANE

KENNYLANDS

GROVE

CHERITON
CL

MAPLE

Liby

Sch

ROAD   DRIVE

PEPPARD

Young
Wood

5

School

Playing
Field

MOOR

KIDMORE LANE

KIDMORE LA

Holly Tree
Farm

WESTLEIGH

ROWAN
CL

BIRCH CL

ILEX

Hag Pits

BIRD

WOOD

CT

Sewage
Works

Bird
Wood

Kidmore End

DRAYS LEA

LANE

CHALKHOUSE

Emmens
Farm

GREEN

Rudgings
Plantation

ESSEX WY

NASH WY

ROAD

B481

6

School

Cemy

COOPERS
PIGHTLE

Vines
Farm

Bur
Wood

Bird in Hand
PH

BUTLERS
ORCHARD

A **B** **C** **D**

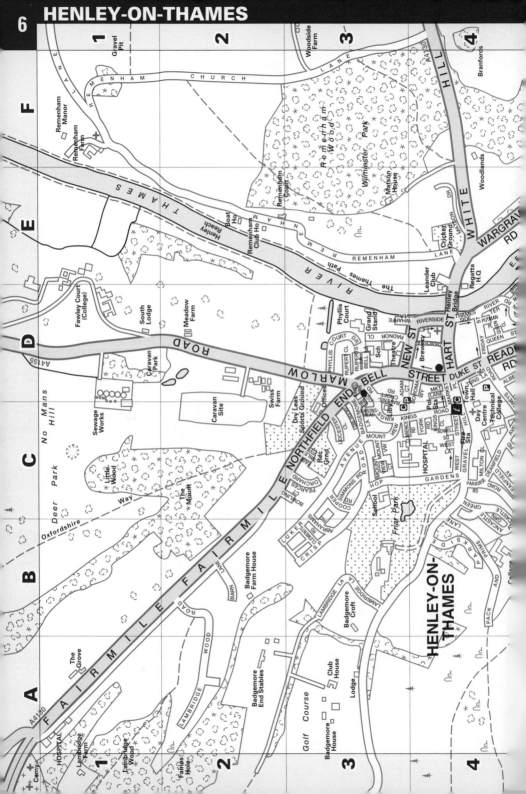

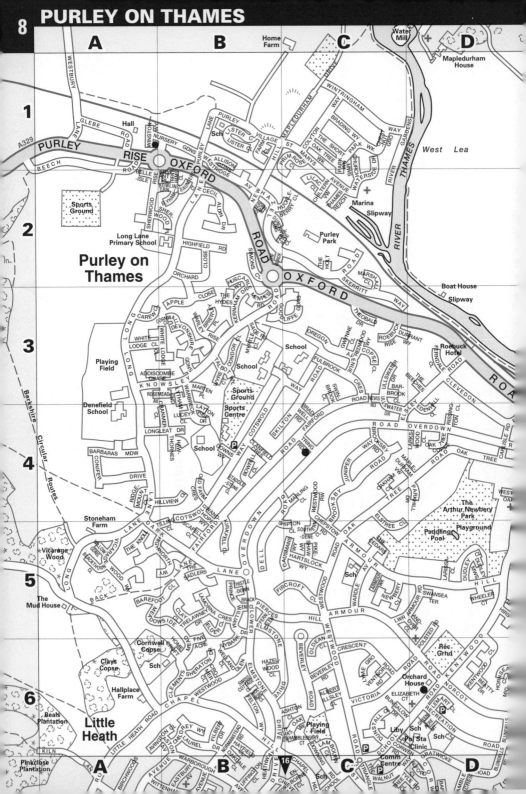

E F G H

Park Wood
Rose Farm
Noke End Shaw
JACKSONS LA
Parkstrings Wood
Sandyhill Plantation
1 The Cottage
Park Farm
Sandy Hill
BLAGRAVE
Blagrave Farm
FARM LANE
JACKSONS
Grain Store
Kings Hill
Chazey Wood
2
BLAGRAVE LANE
10
New Farm
THE
WARREN
Gravel Hill
HEWEN
CHAZEY RD
BLAGRAVE LANE
UPPER WARREN AV UPPER
3
The Warren
Boat House
Kentwood
WARREN THE
TILEHURST
Deeps
Chazey Court Farm
The Chase
The Fishery
Boat Ho
St Marys Island
OXFORD
GRASMERE
Poplar Island
Bucks Stream
Thames Path
4
ROAD
COMISTON DR RYDAL
THIRLMERE
AVENUE
FOREST HL
SAND
RISE
AVE
OXFORD RD IND EST
GRESHAM
DEACON
Appletree Eyot
Upper Large
Norcot Scours
Scours
St Marys Island
Little Johns Farm
5
WEALD AV
Sch
CRANL
BOURNE GDNS
RIVER THAMES
Riverside Caravan Park
Sports Ground
Club
LOVER
18
Clinic
RINGWOOD RD
ROMSEY
Supermarket
WAY
Scourslane Junction
THIRLMERE
LYNDHURST
RIPLEY RD
ROMSEY GDNS
SE BOURNE GDNS
STADIUM
Depot
STADIUM WAY INDUSTRIAL ESTATE
WAY
PORTMAN
LOVEROCK
LA
JOHNS LANE
ROAD PORTMA
Mc Ilroy Park
KINSON RD
ROCK BOURNE GDNS
BRAMSHAW
WIGMORE
STONE
WIGMORE LANE
CAXTON CL
BROUGH TOM CL
ALBURY
Tilehurst
ROMANY
ROAD
OXFORD
WESTBROOK RD
THORNTON RD THORNTON MWS RYL
6 CATTLE HOSPITA (non casua
Round Copse
BROOMFIELD RD
GLENROSA RD
MILWARD
MOWBRAY DR
EDGAR
NORCOT
DULNAN CL
MORRISON
READING RETAIL PARK
Superstore
CONST
TIDMARSH RD
STREET
LEDBURY RD
TUTOR CR
DORSET RD
GORDON
ALMA ST
SHERWOOD
FIL MEAD STONE
ROAD
Upcroft School
TYLERS PL
AV
LAWRENCE RD
DEVERON DR
THURS
CRAIG AVENUE
STRATHY CL
DON CL
ROWE
DRAYTON
GROVELANDS RD
SHAFTESBURY
ST GEORGES
ST GEORGES RD
BEECHAM GDNS
ALBURY GDNS
CHESTER STREET
ROAD
A329
E **F** **17** **G** **H**
Comparts Plantation
Commun Centre
BRISBANE RD
HELMSDALE RD
Library
OXF
School

The Warren
The Chase

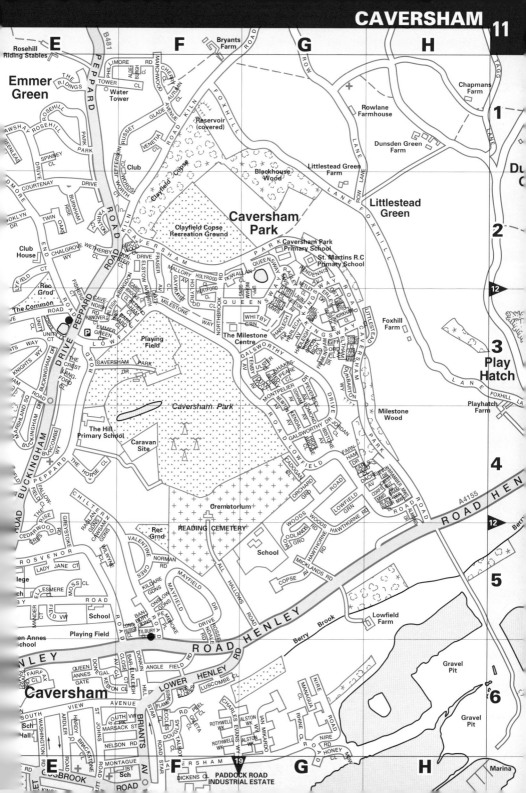

A B C D

1

Chapmans
Farm

Bints
Farm

The
Firs

Ash
Copse

Hampstead
Bottom

Round
Wood

Dunsden
Farmhouse

Spanhill
Copse

Dunsden
Green

Berry Brook

2

Pool
Spring

ROAD HENLEY

SPRING

Botany
Bay

11

Quarry

Sonning Reach

3

Play
Hatch

Homestead
Cottages

FOXHILL LANE

FOXHILL CL.

PLAYHATCH

LANE

NEW ROAD

Sonning
Eye

Playhatch
Farm

B478

Gravel
Works

Hotel

4

ROAD HENLEY

A4155

MARSH LANE

Berry Brook

NEW ROAD

ROAD

Frizers
Farm

Mill
Theatre

SONNING BRIDGE

Sonnin

Hotel

Sailing
Club

Mill
House

THAMES ST.

11

The
Deanery

HIGH ST.

5

Water Ski
Jump

Weir

Lock

Bishops Palace
(site of)

Bishops
Close

PEARSON

The
Dell

Holme Park

LA SONNING

Klog Geo
Field

avel
Pit

RIVER THAMES

Reading
Blue Coat
School

Rifle
Range

Sports
Ground

6

Gravel
Pit

Inglewood
Farm

Sports
Ground

B4446

Sports Ground

Marina

Water
Meadows

Nature Reserve

20 Sonning
Hill

Home Park
Farm

ROAD

THAMES

A B C D

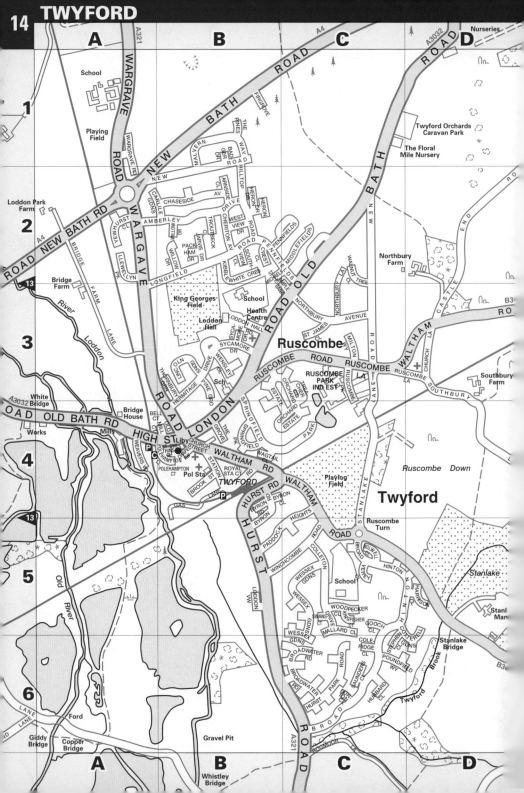

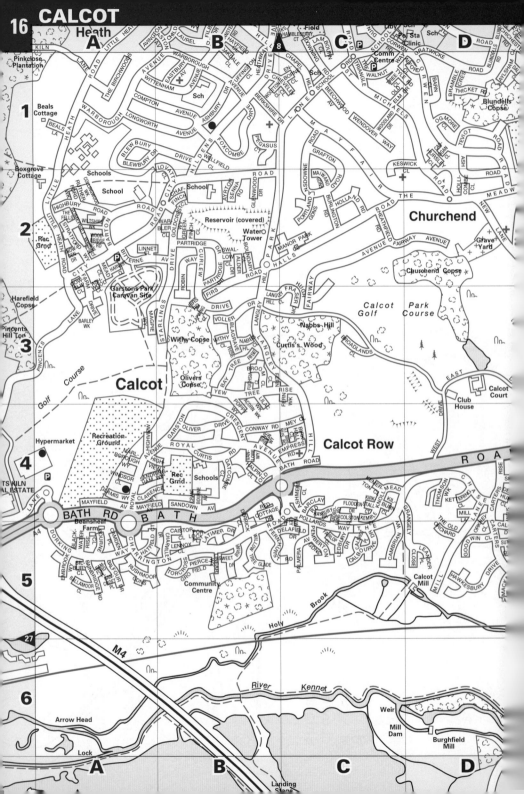

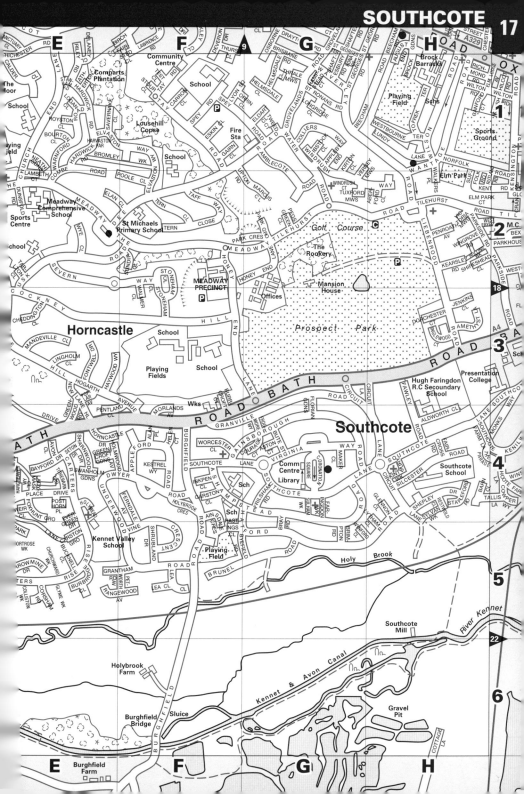

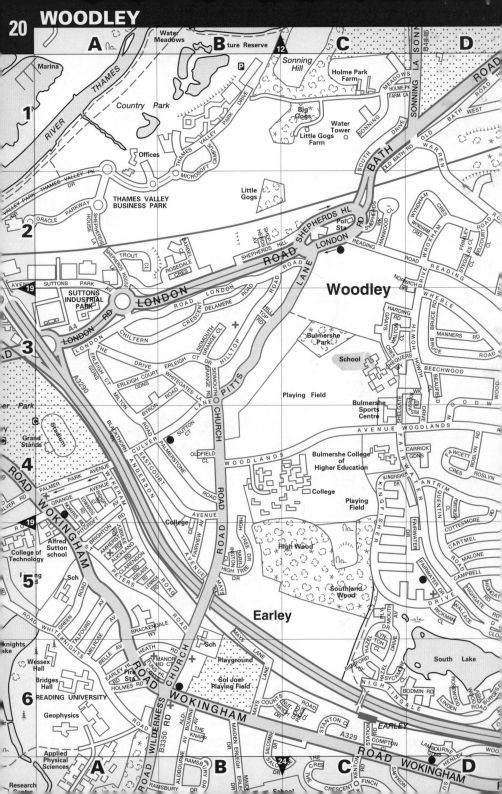

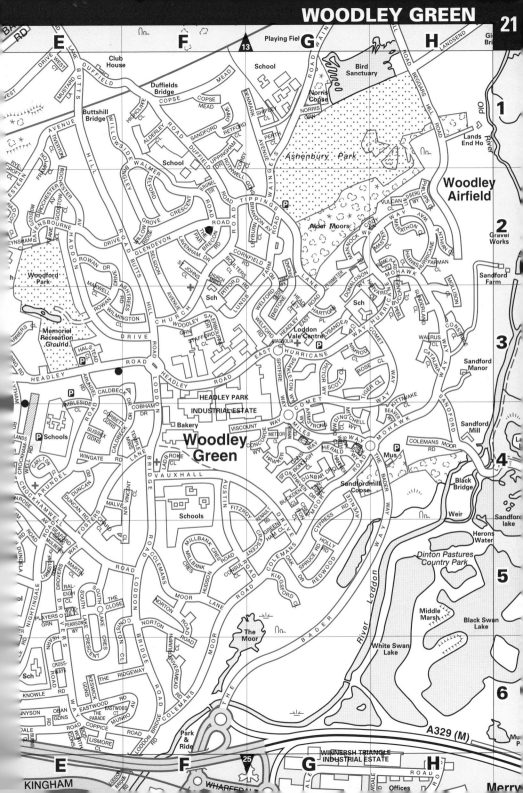

South
Jun
A

Holy Brook
Kennet & Avon Canal
River Kennet
17

B

18

C

Fobney Meadow

ROSE KILN LA
ROSE
A33
ROSE KILN

River Kennet
CRADDOCK
BOULTON RD
DILTON RD
PARKWRIGHT

Water Treatment
Wprks
Fish Farm
Lock
Weir
ISLAND
Manor Farm Cottages

ROSE KILN
HYPERI
WY

BRUNEL
RETAIL PARK
Superste

RELIEF ROAD

Filter Beds
The Mic
Centre

Refuse Disposal Centre

Gravel Pit

Sludge Beds (disused)

Smallmead Stadium

READING

Sewage Purification Works

MANOR FARM

Factory

Filter Beds

COMMERCIAL ROAD

DARWIN CL

SMALLMEAD RD

AVENUE

Whitley

BENNET

ACRE

ROAD

LONGWATER

Brook

DRIVE

Foundry

Northern Wy

HOOPS WY

SHOOTERS WY

READING GATE RETAIL PARK

ACRE ROAD BUSINESS PARK

Recreatio
Groun

C

GREEN

PARK

SMALL MEAD RD

ROYAL W

Madejski Stadium
READING F.C.

BOOT END

BISCUIT WY

HURST

SHOOTERS WY

WAY

WORTON DR

The Post House Hotel

M4

AVENUE

SOUTH

BROOK

SOUTH OAK WAY

OAK WAY

SOUTH OAK WAY

WORTON GRANGE INDUSTRIAL ESTATE

RELIEF

IMPERIAL

Brewery

PINGEWOOD ROAD SOUTH

Hartley Court Farm

Hartley Court

HARTLEY COURT ROAD

28

HARTLEY COURT

BASINGSTO

ROAD

Hopkiln Farm

A

B

C

D

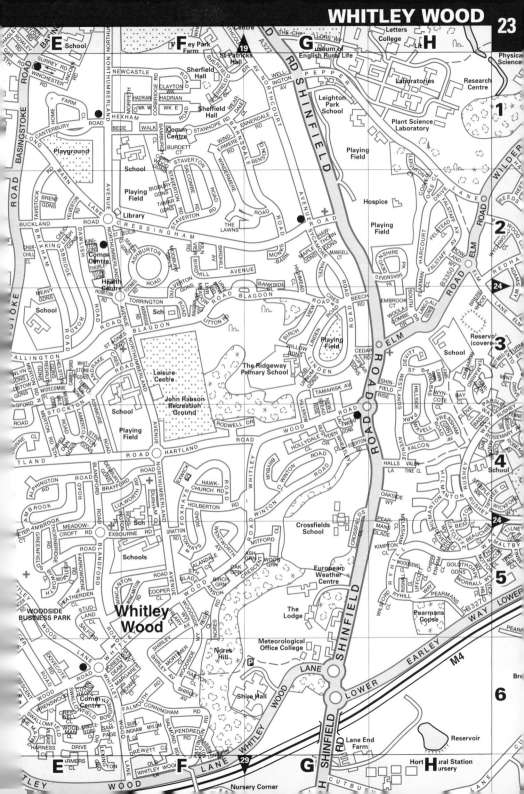

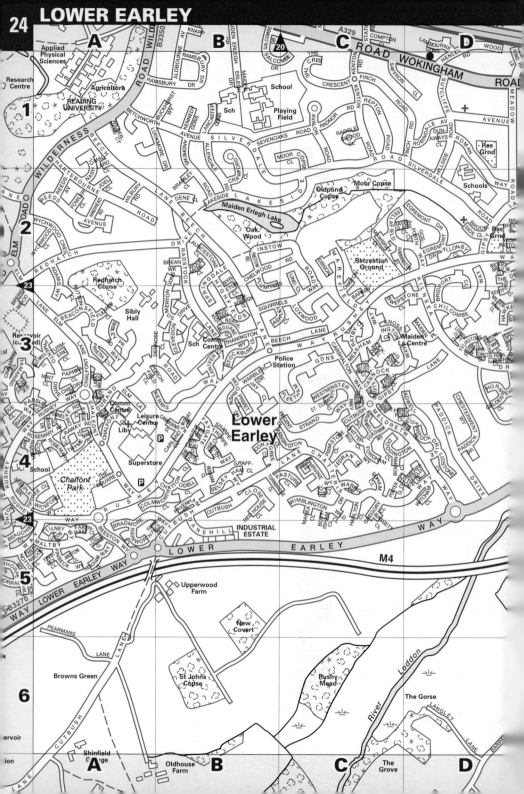

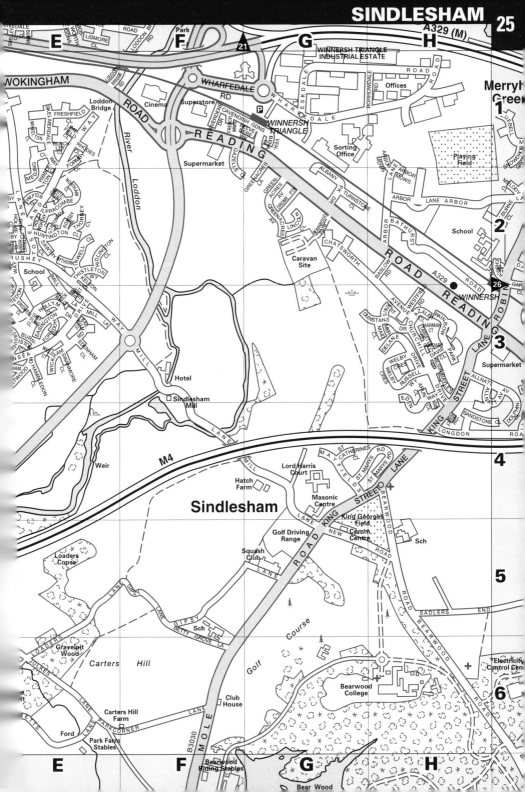

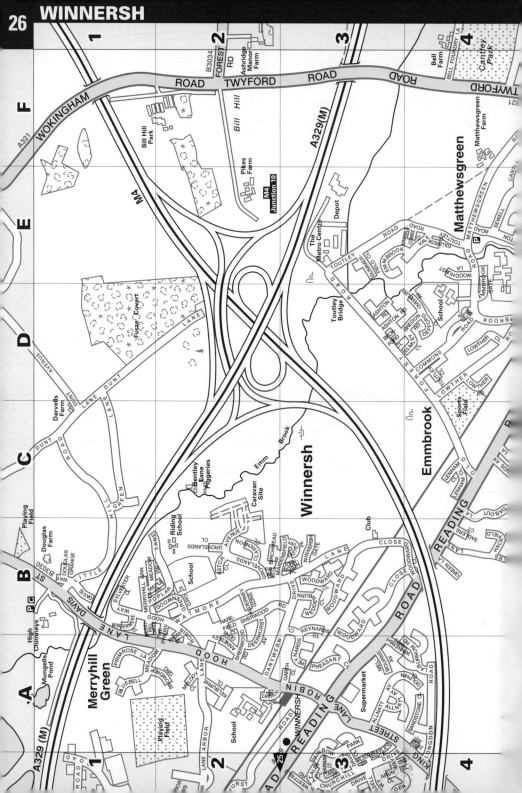

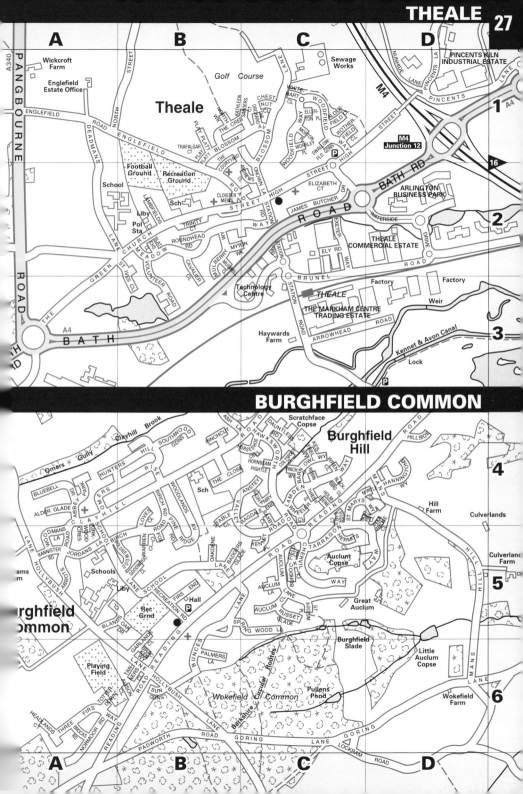

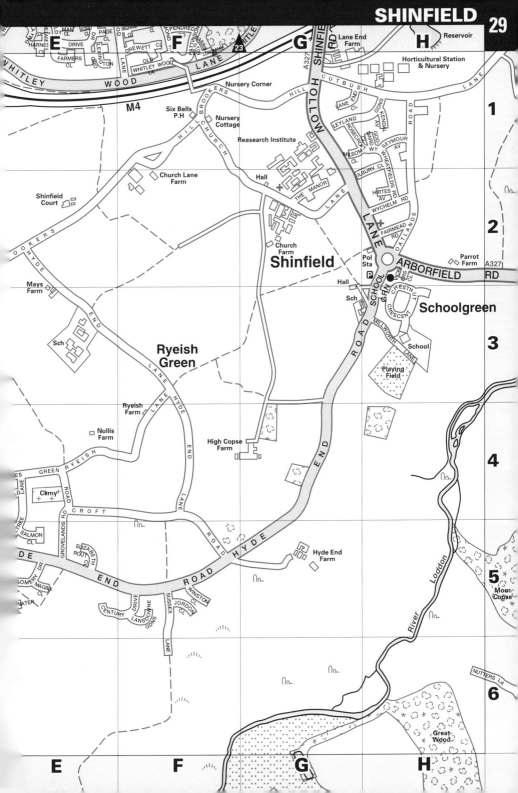

The Index includes some names for which there is insufficient space on the maps. These names are preceded by an * and are followed by the nearest adjoining thoroughfare.

BURGHFIELD COMMON

Abbey Pk RG7 — 27 A4
Abbots Rd RG7 — 27 A5
Alder Glade RG7 — 27 A4
Alison Cl RG7 — 27 B6
Anstey Pl RG7 — 27 C4
Ash La RG7 — 27 B4
Auclum Cl RG7 — 27 C5
Auclum La RG7 — 27 C5

Badgers Glade RG7 — 27 B5
Bannister Rd RG7 — 27 A5
Barn Owl Way RG7 — 27 C4
Birch Rd RG7 — 27 A5
Blackbird Cl RG7 — 27 C4
Blands Cl RG7 — 27 A5
Bluebell Cl RG7 — 27 A4
Boldrewood RG7 — 27 B5
Bracken Way RG7 — 27 B6
Brocas Rd RG7 — 27 A6
Bunces La RG7 — 27 B6
Burdock Cl RG7 — 27 C5

Chervil Way RG7 — 27 C5
Clayhill Rd RG7 — 27 A4
Coltsfoot Cl RG7 — 27 C4

Dauntless Rd RG7 — 27 C4

Field Cl RG7 — 27 C5
Finch Way RG7 — 27 C4
Firs End RG7 — 27 B5
Fox Cl RG7 — 27 B5

Garlands Cl RG7 — 27 B6
Goodwood Cl RG7 — 27 B5
Goring La RG7 — 27 B6
Granby End RG7 — 27 C4
Great Auclum Pl RG7 — 27 C5

Hanningtons Way RG7 — 27 D4
Hawksworth Rd RG7 — 27 C4
Hermits Cl RG7 — 27 C5
Highfield Cl RG7 — 27 C4
Hillside RG7 — 27 D4
Hollybush La RG7 — 27 A4
Holmedene RG7 — 27 C4
Hornbeam Pightle RG7 — 27 C4
Horseshoe Cres RG7 — 27 B4
Hunters Hill RG7 — 27 A4

Jordans La RG7 — 27 A5

Kennet Pl RG7 — 27 C5
Kestrel Way RG7 — 27 C4
Kirkwood Cres RG7 — 27 A5

Lamden Way RG7 — 27 C4
Lockram Rd RG7 — 27 C6
Loves Cl RG7 — 27 B4

Mans Hill RG7 — 27 D4
Myrtle Cl RG7 — 27 C4

Normoor Rd RG7 — 27 A6

Oak Dr RG7 — 27 B5
Oakdene RG7 — 27 B5
Omers Rise RG7 — 27 A4

Padworth Rd RG7 — 27 B6
Palmers La RG7 — 27 B6
Pembroke Cl RG7 — 27 D5
Pinchcut RG7 — 27 B4
Pine Ridge Rd RG7 — 27 B4

Ragdale RG7 — 27 C4
Reading Rd RG7 — 27 A6
Recreation Rd RG7 — 27 B5
Robin Cl RG7 — 27 B5
Russet Glade RG7 — 27 C5

St Marys Way RG7 — 27 C4
Saxby Cl RG7 — 27 C4
School La RG7 — 27 B5
Sorrel Cl RG7 — 27 C4
Southwood Gdns RG7 — 27 B4
Springwood La RG7 — 27 B5
Stable Cl RG7 — 27 B5
Sun Gdns RG7 — 27 B6

Tanners Cl RG7 — 27 B6
Tarragon Way RG7 — 27 C5
The Close RG7 — 27 B4
Three Firs Way RG7 — 27 A6
Thrush Cl RG7 — 27 C4
Totterdown RG7 — 27 A6

Valley Rd RG7 — 27 B4

Warren Cl RG7 — 27 B5
Wheeler Cl RG7 — 27 C4
Woodlands Av RG7 — 27 B4
Woodmans La RG7 — 27 A5
Wren Cl RG7 — 27 C4

HENLEY ON THAMES

Abrahams Rd RG9 — 6 B3
Adam Ct RG9 — 6 D3
Adwell Sq RG9 — 6 C4
Albert Rd RG9 — 6 D4
Ancastle Grn RG9 — 6 B4
Auton Pl RG9 — 7 C6

Badgemore La RG9 — 6 C3
Barn La RG9 — 6 B2
Baronsmead RG9 — 6 C3
Bell La RG9 — 6 D3
Bell St RG9 — 6 D3
Belle Vue Rd RG9 — 7 C6
Berkshire Rd RG9 — 7 C6
Blandy Rd RG9 — 7 C6
Boathouse Reach RG9 — 7 E5
Boroma Way RG9 — 6 C4
Boston Rd RG9 — 7 D6
Bowling Ct RG9 — 6 C3

Carlesgill Pl RG9 — 7 D6
Chalcraft Cl RG9 — 7 B6
Chalk Hill RG9 — 7 A8
Chiltern Cl RG9 — 7 A5
Church Av RG9 — 6 D4
Church St RG9 — 7 D5
Clarence Rd RG9 — 6 C4
Clements Rd RG9 — 6 B3
Coldharbour Cl RG9 — 7 B6

Cooper Rd RG9 — 6 C3
Crisp Rd RG9 — 6 B3
Cromwell Cl RG9 — 7 C6
Cromwell Rd RG9 — 7 D6

Damer Gdns RG9 — 7 D6
Deanfield Av RG9 — 6 C4
Deanfield Rd RG9 — 7 B5
Drawback Hill RG9 — 7 C7
Duke St RG9 — 6 D4

Elizabeth Cl RG9 — 7 A5
Elizabeth Rd RG9 — 7 A5

Fairmile RG9 — 6 A1
Fairmile Ct RG9 — 6 C3
Farm Rd RG9 — 7 E6
Friday St RG9 — 6 D4

Gainsborough Cres RG9 — 7 B5
Gainsborough Hill RG9 — 7 C5
Gainsborough Rd RG9 — 7 C5
Gillotts Cl RG9 — 7 A6
Gillotts La RG9 — 7 A6
Grange Rd RG9 — 7 D5
Gravel Hill RG9 — 6 C4
Gravett Cl RG9 — 7 B5
Green La RG9 — 7 C6
Greys Hill RG9 — 7 C5
Greys Rd RG9 — 6 C4
Grove Rd RG9 — 7 D5

Hamilton Av RG9 — 7 D5
Harcourt Cl RG9 — 7 B5
Harpsden Rd RG9 — 7 D5
Harpsden Way RG9 — 7 D6
Hart St RG9 — 6 D4
Haywards RG9 — 7 B5
Hewgate Ct RG9 — 6 D4
Homelands Way RG9 — 7 C6
Hop Gdns RG9 — 6 C3

INDUSTRIAL & RETAIL:
Fairview Industrial Est RG9 — 7 E5

King James Way RG9 — 7 B6
Kings Cl RG9 — 6 C4
Kings Rd RG9 — 6 C3
Kings Walk RG9 — 6 D3
Knappe Cl RG9 — 7 B5

Lambridge La RG9 — 6 B3
Lambridge Wood Rd RG9 — 6 A2
Lauds Cl RG9 — 7 B5
Leaver Rd RG9 — 7 C5
Leicester Cl RG9 — 6 C3
Lovell Cl RG9 — 7 B6
Luker Av RG9 — 6 B2

Makins Rd RG9 — 7 A6
Manor Rd RG9 — 7 C6
Market La RG9 — 6 D4
Market Pl RG9 — 6 C4
Marlow Rd RG9 — 6 C4
Marmion Rd RG9 — 7 D5
Matson Dr RG9 — 6 E4
Meadow Rd RG9 — 6 D4
Mill La RG9 — 7 E6
Milton Cl RG9 — 6 C4
Mount View RG9 — 6 C3
Mount View Ct RG9 — 6 C3

New St RG9 — 6 D3
Newtown Gdns RG9 — 7 D6
Newtown Rd RG9 — 7 E6
Niagara Rd RG9 — 7 D6
Nicholas Rd RG9 — 7 A6
Norman Av RG9 — 7 D5
Northfield Cl RG9 — 6 C3
Northfield End RG9 — 6 C3

Orchard Cl RG9 — 7 D5

Pack And Prime La RG9 — 6 B4
Paradise Rd RG9 — 6 B4
Park Rd RG9 — 7 D5
Parkside RG9 — 6 B4
Pearces Orch RG9 — 6 C3
Peppard La RG9 — 7 C6
Periam Cl RG9 — 7 B5
Perseverance Hill RG9 — 7 A8
Phyllis Court Dr RG9 — 6 D3
Putman Pl RG9 — 6 D4

Quebec Rd RG9 — 7 D5
Queen Cl RG9 — 6 D4
Queen St RG9 — 6 D4

Radnor Cl RG9 — 6 D3
Ravenscroft Rd RG9 — 6 D3
Reading Rd RG9 — 6 D4
Remenham Church La RG9 — 6 F1
Remenham La RG9 — 6 E3
River Ter RG9 — 6 D4
Riverside RG9 — 6 D4
Rotherfield Rd RG9 — 7 C7
Rupert Cl RG9 — 6 D3
Ruperts La RG9 — 6 D3

St Andrews Rd RG9 — 7 B6
St Annes Cl RG9 — 7 C5
St Katherines Rd RG9 — 7 C6
St Marks Rd RG9 — 7 C6
Sherwood Gdns RG9 — 7 B6
Simmons Rd RG9 — 6 C3
Singers Cl RG9 — 7 D5
Singers La RG9 — 7 D5
South Av RG9 — 7 D6
Station Rd RG9 — 6 D4
Stow Rd RG9 — 7 E5

Thames Side RG9 — 6 D4
The Close RG9 — 7 C5
The Hocket RG9 — 6 C3
Tilebarn Cl RG9 — 7 B5
Tilebarn La RG9 — 7 B5
Trinity Cl RG9 — 7 C5
Trust Corner RG9 — 7 D6
Tuns La RG9 — 6 D4
Two Tree Hill RG9 — 7 A5

Upton Cl RG9 — 7 D5

Valley Rd RG9 — 7 A6
Vicarage Rd RG9 — 7 D5
Victoria Ct RG9 — 7 D5

Walton Av RG9 — 7 D5
War Memorial Pl RG9 — 7 D6
Wargrave Rd RG9 — 6 E4
Watermans Rd RG9 — 7 D6
West La RG9 — 6 C4
West St RG9 — 6 C4
Western Av RG9 — 7 D6
Western Rd RG9 — 7 D5
Wharfe La RG9 — 6 D3
Whitamore Row RG9 — 7 D6

White Hill RG9 — 6 E4
Wilson Av RG9 — 7 D6
Woodlands Rd RG9 — 7 C6
Wootton Rd RG9 — 7 B6
Wyndale Cl RG9 — 7 D6

York Rd RG9 — 6 C4

LOWER SHIPLAKE / WARGRAVE

Autumn Walk RG10 — 15 D

Backsideans RG10 — 15 D
Badgers Walk RG9 — 15 A
Baskerville La RG9 — 15 A
Basmore La RG9 — 15 D
Bayliss Rd RG10 — 15 D
Beverley Gdns RG10 — 15
Blakes Rd RG10 — 15 A
Bolney La RG9 — 15 A
Bolney Rd RG9 — 15
Bolney Trevor Dr RG9 — 15 A
Brampton Chase RG9 — 15
Braybrooke Gdns RG10 — 15
Braybrooke Rd RG10 — 15
Brocks Way RG9 — 15

Church St RG10 — 15
Clifton Rise RG10 — 15
Crowsley Rd RG10 — 15

Dark La RG10 — 15
Dunnock Way RG10 — 15

East View Cl RG10 — 15
East View Rd RG10 — 15
Elizabeth Ct RG10 — 15
Emma La RG10 — 15

Ferry La RG10 — 15
Fidlers Walk RG10 — 15

Hamilton Rd RG10 — 15
Henley Rd RG10 — 15
High St RG10 — 15
Highfield Pk RG10 — 15
Hillands RG10 — 15

Langhams Way RG10 — 15
Lashbrook Mead RG9 — 15
Lashbrook Rd RG9 — 15
Loddon Dr RG10 — 15
Lowes Cl RG9 — 15

Manor Wood Gate RG9 — 15
McCraes Walk RG10 — 15
Mill La RG9 — 15
Mill Rd RG9 — 15
Mumbery Hill RG10 — 15

New Rd RG9 — 15
Newalls Rise RG10 — 15
Northfield Av RG9 — 15
Northfield Rd RG9 — 15
Nursery Cl RG9 — 15

Oaks Rd RG9 — 15

Purfield Dr RG10 — 15

Quarry La RG9 — 15

eading Rd RG9 15 A1
ecreation Rd RG10 15 E3
idgeway RG10 15 E3
yecroft Cl RG10 15 E3

chool Hill RG10 15 E4
chool La RG10 15 D4
ilverdale Rd RG10 15 D4
pring Walk RG10 15 D4
tation Rd,
Shiplake RG9 15 A1
tation Rd,
Wargrave RG10 15 C4

he Bothy RG10 15 D3
he Chestnuts RG9 15 A2
he Copse RG10 15 E3
he Crescent RG9 15 B2
he Spur RG10 15 E3
he Vinery RG10 15 D3
he Walled Gdn
RG10 15 D3
yford Rd RG10 15 D4

ctoria Rd RG10 15 E4

argrave Hill RG10 15 D3
atermans Way
field RG10 15 C4
estfield Cres RG9 15 B2
llow La RG9 15 C1
oodlands Rd RG9 15 A2

PANGBOURNE

on Cl RG8 4 C3

e Court Rd RG8 4 A5
rne Rd RG8 4 C3
edons Hill RG8 4 B3
rs Cl RG8 4 D3
knell Av RG8 4 C3

ar Dr RG8 4 B4
tern Walk RG8 4 C3
rch Rd RG8 4 D3
ch House Ct RG8 4 C3
rtlands Hill RG8 4 B4

hess Cl RG8 4 B1
luce Gdns RG8 4 C3

field La RG8 4 B1

ers Hill RG8 4 B4

ame Av RG8 4 C4
n La RG8 4 A4

wick Rd RG8 4 B3
slock Ct RG8 4 A2
St,
ngbourne RG8 4 B3
St,
itchurch on Thames
8 4 B1
de RG8 4 C1
eshoe Pk RG8 4 C3
shoe Rd RG8 4 C3

STRIAL & RETAIL:
eshoe Pk
ustrial Est RG8 4 C4

edy Dr RG8 4 C4

r Rd RG8 4 B1
ow La RG8 4 C3
owside Rd RG8 4 C3
Gdns RG8 4 C3

Pangbourne Hill RG8 4 A4
Pangbourne Mews
RG8 4 C3
Purley Rise RG8 4 D3
Purley Way RG8 4 C3

Reading Rd RG8 4 B3
Riverview Rd RG8 4 B3

St James Cl RG8 4 B3
Shooters Hill RG8 4 A2
Short St RG8 4 C3
Station Rd RG8 4 B3
Stokes Vw RG8 4 B3
Strachay Cl RG8 4 B6
Sulham La RG8 4 D4
Swanston Field RG8 4 B1
Sycamore Ct RG8 4 B3

Thames Av RG8 4 B2
The Laurels RG8 4 C3
The Moors RG8 4 B3
The Square RG8 4 B3
The Street RG8 4 B5
The Wharf RG8 4 B2
Tidmarsh La RG8 4 A6
Tidmarsh Rd RG8 4 B4

Whitchurch Rd RG8 4 B2
Wilder Av RG8 4 D3
Willow Ct RG8 4 B3
Woodview Rd RG8 4 C3

READING

Abattoirs Rd RG1 3 B1
Abbey Sq RG1 3 D3
Abbey St RG1 3 D2
Abbots Walk RG1 3 D2
Aberaman RG4 10 C2
Aberford Cl RG30 17 H2
Abingdon Dr RG4 11 F3
Acacia Rd RG1 19 F4
Acorn Walk RG31 16 B3
Acre Rd RG2 22 C4
Adams Way RG6 24 A2
Addington Rd RG1 19 F5
Addiscombe Chase
RG31 8 A3
Addison Rd RG1 3 B1
Adelaide Rd RG6 20 A5
Admirals Ct RG1 18 D5
Adwell Dr RG6 24 C5
Ainsdale Cres RG30 17 F4
Alan Pl RG30 17 F4
Alandale Cl RG2 23 F5
Albany Park Dr RG41 25 G2
Albany Rd RG30 18 A3
Albert Illsley Cl RG31 8 C6
Albert Rd RG4 10 B4
Albion Ter RG1 3 E4
Albury Cl RG30 9 H6
Albury Gdns RG4 17 E5
Aldbourne Av RG6 20 B6
Aldeburgh Cl RG4 11 F1
Aldenham Cl RG4 11 F3
Alder Cl RG6 24 D3
Alder Dr RG31 16 B2
Alderley Cl RG5 21 F1
Alderney Gdns RG41 26 B2
Aldworth Cl RG30 17 H4
Alexandra Rd RG1 19 G4
Alford Cl RG30 16 D1
Alfred St RG1 3 B3
All Hallows Rd RG4 11 F5
Allcroft Rd RG1 19 E5
Allendale Rd RG6 24 B1
Allison Gdns RG8 8 B1
Allnatt Av RG41 26 A3
Allonby Cl RG6 24 D2

Alma St RG30 9 H6
Almond Dr RG4 11 H4
Alphington Rd RG2 23 E4
Alpine St RG1 18 D5
Alston Walk RG4 11 G6
Amblecote Rd RG30 17 G1
Ambleside Cl RG5 21 E4
Ambrook Rd RG2 23 E4
Ambrose Pl RG1 3 A3
Amersham Rd RG4 19 F1
Amethyst La RG30 17 H3
Amherst Rd RG6 20 A5
Amity Rd RG1 19 G3
Amity St RG1 19 G3
Ammanford RG4 10 B3
Anderson Av RG6 20 A4
Andover Cl RG31 8 D5
Andrews Rd RG6 20 D6
Angle Field Rd RG4 11 F6
Anglers Way RG1 3 F3
Angus Cl RG31 16 D4
Annesley Gdns RG41 26 A2
Anson Cres RG2 23 F5
Anstey Rd RG1 3 B3
Anston Cl RG2 24 A5
Anthian Cl RG5 21 H2
Antrim Rd RG5 20 D4
Antrim Rd RG5 21 E4
Anvil Cl RG7 28 D5
Apple Cl RG31 8 B3
Appleby End RG30 17 G1
Appleford Rd RG30 17 F4
Appletree La RG7 29 E5
Arbor La RG41 25 H1
Arbor Mdws RG41 25 H1
Arborfield Rd RG2 29 H2
Arbour Cl RG1 18 C6
Ardler Rd RG4 11 E6
Argyle Rd RG1 18 B3
Argyle St RG1 18 B3
Arkwright Rd RG2 22 D1
Armadale Ct RG30 18 A4
Armour Hill RG31 8 C5
Armour Rd RG31 8 C5
Armour Walk RG31 8 C5
Armstrong Way RG5 21 G4
Arthur Pl RG1 3 F3
Arun Cl RG41 25 H3
Arundel Rd RG5 21 E3
Ash Grn RG2 23 G5
Ash Rd RG30 16 D1
Ashampstead Rd
RG30 17 F4
Ashburton Rd RG2 23 F2
Ashbury Dr RG31 16 B1
Ashby Ct RG2 23 E5
Ashcroft Cl RG4 10 B3
Ashley Cl RG6 24 B3
Ashley Rd RG1 18 B5
Ashmere Cl RG6 16 C4
Ashmere Ter RG30 18 A2
Ashmore Rd RG2 23 E3
Ashton Cl RG31 8 B6
Ashton Rd RG41 26 D3
Ashtrees Rd RG5 21 E3
Ashwood RG5 20 D6
Ashwood Cl RG31 16 A2
Askew Dr RG7 28 D4
Aston Av RG31 8 B6
Aston Ct RG30 17 G4
Astor Cl RG41 26 B2
Atherton Cl RG30 17 E1
Auburn Ct RG4 10 C6
Auckland Rd RG6 20 A5
Audley St RG30 18 A2
August End RG30 17 H1
Austin Rd RG5 21 F4
Autumn Cl RG4 11 F1
Avalon Rd RG6 24 C1
Avebury Sq RG1 19 G5
Aveley Walk RG2 19 E5
Avington Cl RG31 8 A6

Avon Cl RG31 17 E4
Avon Pl RG1 19 G3
Axbridge Rd RG2 23 F3
Aylsham Cl RG30 16 D1
Ayrton Senna Rd
RG31 16 B2
Azalea Cl RG41 25 H3

Babbington Rd RG2 23 F6
Back La RG31 8 A5
Badgers Rise RG4 10 C4
Bainbridge Rd RG31 16 A5
Baker St RG1 3 A3
Baker St RG1 18 B4
Balfour Dr RG31 16 A5
Ballamoor Cl RG31 16 A5
Balliol Rd RG4 10 A5
Balme Cl RG10 13 G5
Balmore Dr RG4 10 D5
Balmore Pk RG4 10 D5
Bamburg Cl RG2 23 F1
Bamford Pl RG31 16 A5
Banbury Gdns RG4 11 F5
Bancroft Pl RG31 16 A5
Bankside Cl RG2 23 G2
Barbaras Mdw RG31 8 A4
Barbel Cl RG2 20 B2
Barbrook Cl RG31 8 C3
Barclay Rd RG31 16 C4
Barclose Av RG4 11 F6
Barefoot Cl RG31 8 B5
Barholm Cl RG6 25 E3
Barkby RG6 24 C3
Barkwith Cl RG6 25 E2
Barley Walk RG31 16 A3
Barn Cl,
Southcote RG30 17 H4
Barn Cl,
Tilehurst RG30 16 D1
Barnard Cl RG4 11 F3
Barnsdale Rd RG2 23 F1
Barnstaple St RG1 18 D4
Barnwood Cl RG30 18 A2
Barnwood Ct RG30 18 A2
Baron Ct RG30 18 A4
Barracks La RG7 28 D5
Barretts La RG2 24 D6
Barrington Cl RG5 20 B5
Barrington Way RG1 18 A5
Barry Pl RG1 3 B1
Barton Rd RG31 16 A2
Basil Cl RG6 23 H4
Basingstoke Rd,
Reading RG2 19 E6
Basingstoke Rd,
Three Mile Cross
RG7 28 D2
Baslow Rd RG41 25 H2
Bassett Cl RG6 24 C4
Bath Rd,
Calcot RG31 16 A4
Bath Rd,
Reading RG1 3 A4
Bath Rd,
Sonning RG4 13 E6
Bathurst Rd RG41 25 H2
Battle St RG1 3 A2
Bay Cl RG6 23 H3
Bay Tree Rise RG31 16 B3
Baydon Dr RG1 18 B5
Bayford Dr RG31 17 E4
Bayley Ct RG41 25 H3
Beaconsfield Way
RG6 24 A3
Bearwood Path RG41 25 G2
Bearwood Rd RG41 25 H4
Beatty Dr RG30 8 D6
Beauchief Cl RG6 23 H5
Beaufield Cl RG6 20 D3
Beaver Way RG5 21 H4
Beck Ct RG1 19 F5
Beckford Cl RG41 26 D3

Bede Walk RG2 23 E1
Bedford Rd RG1 3 A2
Beech Hill Rd RG7 28 C6
Beech La RG6 24 A1
Beech Rd,
Purley-on-Thames
RG8 8 A2
Beech Rd,
Reading RG2 23 G3
Beech Rd,
Tokers Green RG4 10 A1
Beecham Rd RG30 17 G1
Beechwood Av,
Tilehurst RG31 16 C1
Beechwood Av,
Woodley RG5 20 D3
Beeston Way RG6 24 A5
Beggers Hill Rd RG10 13 H6
Beighton Cl RG6 23 H5
Belle Av RG6 20 A6
Belle Vue Rd RG1 3 A4
Belle Vue Ter RG1 18 B4
Belleisle RG8 8 A2
Bellingham Walk RG4 10 D3
Bellvedere Walk RG41 25 F1
Belmont Rd RG30 18 A4
Bembridge Pl RG1 3 E3
Bennet Rd RG2 22 C4
Benson Ct RG2 23 G1
Benyon Cl RG1 18 B5
Benyon Ct Mews RG1 18 B5
Beresford Rd RG30 18 A3
Berkeley Av RG1 18 A5
Berkeley Ct RG1 3 A4
Berkshire Dr RG31 16 B1
Berrylands Rd RG4 10 D6
Berstead Cl RG6 24 B4
Betam Rd RG1 3 F3
Betchworth Av RG6 24 A1
Betty Grove La RG41 25 F5
Beverley Rd RG31 8 C6
Bexley Ct RG30 18 A4
Bibury Cl RG5 20 D6
Bideford Cl RG5 20 C6
Bigbury Gdns RG2 23 F2
Biko Ct RG1 3 F3
Binbrook Way RG6 24 D2
Bingley Gro RG5 21 F1
Birch Av RG30 9 E6
Birch Grn RG2 23 F5
Birch Vw RG2 23 G3
Birchmead RG41 26 B2
Birchwood Cl RG4 11 F2
Birdhill Av RG2 23 F2
Birkhall Cl RG31 16 C4
Biscuit Way RG2 22 C4
Bishops Rd RG6 20 A4
Bitterne Av RG31 16 A2
Blackley Cl RG6 25 E1
Blackthorn Cl,
Earley RG6 20 A4
Blackthorn Cl,
Tilehurst RG31 8 A5
Blackwater Cl,
Caversham RG4 11 H4
Blackwater Cl,
Spencers Wood
RG7 29 E5
Blackwater Rise RG31 16 A5
Blaenant RG4 10 C3
Blaenavon RG4 10 C3
Blagdon Rd RG2 23 F3
Blagrave Farm La
RG4 9 H1
Blagrave La RG4 9 H1
Blagrave Rise RG31 16 B3
Blagrave St RG1 3 C2
Blakes Cotts RG3 3 E3
Blanchard Cl RG5 21 H2
Blandford Rd RG2 23 E4
Blenheim Gdns RG1 19 G5

Blenheim Rd, Caversham RG4 10 C5
Blenheim Rd, Reading RG1 19 G4
Blewbury Dr RG31 16 A1
Bloomfieldhatch La RG7 28 A5
Bluebell Mdw RG41 26 A1
Blundells Rd RG30 16 D1
Blyth Walk RG2 19 E5
Bobgreen Ct RG2 23 E6
Bodmin Rd RG5 20 C6
Body Rd RG1 3 B3
Boot End RG2 22 B5
Borrowdale Rd RG41 25 H1
Bosham Cl RG6 24 A4
Boston Av RG2 18 C5
Bosworth Gdns RG5 21 E6
Bottisham Cl RG6 24 C5
Boult St RG1 3 E4
Boulters Cl RG5 21 F2
Boulton Rd RG2 22 D1
Boults Walk RG2 19 E6
Boundary Cl RG31 16 B2
Boundary La RG4 10 B5
Bourn Cl RG6 24 C4
Bourne Av RG2 19 E6
Bourne Cl RG31 16 A5
Bourne Stevens Cl RG1 3 D3
Bourton Cl RG30 17 E1
Bowfell Cl RG31 8 B4
Bowling Grn La RG8 8 B2
Bracken Cl RG31 8 B5
Brackendale Way RG6 20 A5
Brackstone Cl RG4 11 G6
Brading Way RG8 8 C1
Bradmore Way RG6 24 A5
Bradwell Rd RG31 8 C4
Bramber Mews RG4 11 H4
Bramble Cres RG30 16 D1
Bramblings RG4 10 B3
Bramley Cl RG6 24 B2
Bramshaw Rd RG30 9 F6
Brandon Av RG5 21 G2
Bray Rd RG30 17 G5
Brayford Rd RG2 23 E4
Brean Walk RG6 24 B2
Brecon Rd RG5 21 F2
Bredon Rd RG41 26 D4
Brendon Rd RG30 8 D5
Brent Gdns RG2 23 E2
Brerewood Rd RG6 23 H3
Briants Av RG4 11 F6
Briar Cl RG4 10 C4
Bridge St, Caversham RG1 18 C1
Bridge St, Reading RG1 3 C3
Bridgewater Cl RG30 9 H6
Bridport Cl RG2 24 D3
Brierley Pl RG31 8 B3
Brigham Rd RG1 18 D1
Brighton Rd RG6 20 A5
Brill Cl RG4 10 C4
Brimblecombe Cl RG41 26 E4
Brimpton Rd RG30 17 G5
Brisbane Rd RG30 9 G6
Britten Rd RG2 18 D6
Brixham Rd RG2 23 E2
Broad St RG1 3 C3
Broadlands Cl RG31 16 C3
Broadmoor La RG4 13 E5
Brock Gdns RG30 17 H1
Brockley Cl RG30 9 F6
Bromley Walk RG30 17 E1
Brompton Cl RG6 24 D3
Brook Dr RG2 22 B5
Brook Lea RG4 19 F1
Brook St West RG1 3 B4

Brookers Hill RG2,7 28 D2
Brooklyn Dr RG4 10 D2
Brooksby Rd RG31 8 C4
*Brookside, Hargreaves Way RG31 17 E4
Brookside Cl RG6 24 D2
Broom Cl RG31 16 B3
Broomfield Rd RG30 9 F6
Broughton Dr RG30 9 H6
Brownlow Rd RG1 18 B4
Bruce Rd RG3 20 D3
Brunel Arcade RG1 3 C2
Brunel Dr RG5 21 F2
Brunel Rd RG30 17 F5
Brunswick Hill RG1 18 A4
Brunswick St RG1 18 B4
Bryant Pl RG8 8 B2
Brybur Cl RG2 23 G4
Buccaneer Cl RG5 21 H3
Buckden Cl RG5 21 G4
Buckhurst Way RG6 24 B1
Buckingham Dr RG4 11 E4
Buckland Rd RG2 23 E2
Bucknell Cl RG31 17 E5
Buckside Rd RG1 10 C6
Bulmershe Rd RG1 19 H4
Bungalow Dr RG31 8 C6
Burbridge Cl RG31 17 E5
Burcombe Way RG4 11 E4
Burdett Ct RG2 23 F1
Burford Ct RG1 3 A2
Burgess Cl RG5 20 D6
Burghfield Rd RG30 17 F4
Burleigh Mews RG4 11 E3
Burlingham Cl RG2 23 F6
Burlington Rd RG30 16 C2
Burnham Rise RG4 11 E2
Burniston Cl RG6 25 E3
Burns Cl RG5 21 F6
Burrcroft Ct RG30 17 F3
Burwell Cl RG6 24 C4
Bute St RG30 17 G4
Butter Market RG1 3 D3
Butts Hill Rd RG5 21 E1
Buxton Av RG4 10 B4
Byefield Rd RG30 17 F5
Byreton Cl RG6 24 B2
Byron Rd RG6 20 A4
Bythorn Cl RG6 25 E2
Byworth Cl RG2 23 E5

Cadogan Cl, Caversham RG4 11 G4
Cadogan Cl, Tilehurst RG30 16 D1
Caistor Cl RG31 16 B5
Calbourne Dr RG31 16 C5
Calcot Place Dr RG31 17 E4
Caldbeck Dr RG5 21 E3
Calder Cl RG30 17 E1
Caleta Cl RG4 11 F6
Callington Rd RG2 23 E3
Calshot Pl RG31 16 C5
Camborne Cl RG6 24 B4
Cambrian Way RG31 16 C5
Cambridge St RG1 18 B3
Camden Pl RG31 16 A5
Camelford Cl RG2 23 E3
Campbell Rd RG5 20 D5
Canal Way RG1 19 F3
Canford Ct RG30 17 H1
Cannock Way RG6 24 C3
Cannon St RG1 18 B3
Canterbury Rd RG2 23 E1
Cantley Cres RG41 26 E4
Caraway Rd RG6 24 A4
Cardiff Mews RG1 3 A1
Cardiff Rd RG1 3 A1
Cardigan Gdns RG1 19 G5
Cardigan Rd RG1 19 G5
Cardinal Cl RG4 18 D1

Carew Cl RG31 8 A3
Carey St RG1 3 B3
Carisbrooke Cl RG4 11 F2
Carland Cl RG6 24 B4
Carlisle Rd RG31 8 D4
Carlton Cl RG5 21 E4
Carlton Rd RG4 10 A3
Carnarvon Rd RG1 19 G4
Caroline Ct RG1 18 B5
Caroline St RG1 3 A2
Carrick Gdns RG5 20 D4
Carron Cl RG30 17 F1
Carsdale Cl RG1 18 B5
Carshalton Way RG6 24 C3
Carston Gro RG31 17 E5
Carters Rise RG31 16 D4
Cartmel Dr RG5 20 D5
Cassia Dr RG6 24 A4
Castle Cres RG1 18 C4
Castle Hill RG1 3 A4
Castle St RG1 3 B4
Catalina Cl RG5 21 H3
Catcliffe Way RG6 23 H5
Catherine St RG30 18 A3
Causmans Way RG31 8 C5
Cavendish Gdns RG41 25 F1
Cavendish Rd RG4 11 E3
Caversham Park Dr RG4 11 E3
Caversham Park Rd RG4 11 F2
*Caversham Wharf, Thames Side RG1 18 D1
Cawsam Gdns RG4 11 E5
Caxton Cl RG30 9 H6
Cecil Aldin Dr RG31 8 B3
Cedar Rd RG2 23 G3
Cedarwood Cres RG4 11 E5
Centurion Cl RG1 3 C4
Century Dr RG7 29 E5
Chaffinch Cl RG31 16 B2
Chagford Rd RG2 23 E4
Chain St RG1 3 C3
Chain St RG1 18 D3
Chalfont Ct RG6 24 A4
Chalfont Way RG6 24 A3
Chalgrove Way RG4 11 E2
Champion Rd RG4 19 E1
Chancery Mews RG1 3 A4
Chapel Hill RG31 8 B6
Chapel La RG7 28 D5
Chard Cl RG5 21 E4
Charles Evans Way RG4 11 F6
Charles St RG1 3 A2
Charndon Cl RG2 19 E5
Charrington Rd RG31 16 A5
Charvil House Rd RG10 13 G4
Charvil La RG4 13 E5
Charville Dr RG31 16 B5
Chatham St RG1 3 A3
Chatsworth Av RG41 25 G2
Chatsworth Cl RG4 11 F3
Chatteris Way RG6 24 C4
Chatton Cl RG6 24 B4
Chaucer Cl RG4 10 D4
Chazey Rd RG4 10 A5
Cheapside RG1 3 B2
Cheddington Cl RG30 17 E3
Chelford Way RG4 10 B4
Chelsea Cl RG30 9 E6
Chelwood Rd RG6 24 B2
Chepstow Rd RG31 8 C4
Chequers Way RG5 20 C3
Cheriton Ct RG1 3 B4
Cherry Cl RG4 11 F1
Cherwell Rd RG4 10 D2
Chester St, Caversham RG4 10 D6

Chester St, Reading RG30 9 H6
Chesterman St RG1 19 E5
Chesterment Way RG6 24 D3
Chestnut Av RG4 11 H4
Chestnut Cres RG2 29 H3
Chestnut Gro RG8 8 C1
Cheviot Dr RG10 13 H4
Chichester Rd RG30 8 D6
Chicory Cl RG6 24 A3
Chieveley Cl RG31 16 B1
Chilcombe Way RG6 24 D3
Childrey Way RG31 8 B6
Chiltern Cres RG6 20 A3
Chiltern Ct RG4 10 D3
Chiltern Dr RG10 13 H4
Chiltern Rd RG4 11 E4
Chiltern Vw RG8 8 C2
Chippenham Cl RG6 23 H5
Chittering Cl RG6 24 A4
Chive Rd RG6 24 A4
Cholmeley Pl RG1 19 G3
Cholmeley Rd RG1 19 G3
Cholmeley Ter RG1 19 G3
Christchurch Ct RG2 19 E6
Christchurch Gdns RG2 19 E6
Christchurch Rd RG2 19 E6
Chudleigh Gdns RG2 23 E2
Church Cl RG41 26 A2
Church End La RG30 17 E2
Church La RG2 29 F1
Church Mews, Purley on Thames RG8 8 C1
Church Mews, Woodley RG5 21 F2
Church Rd, Caversham RG4 10 C6
Church Rd, Earley RG6 20 B4
Church Rd, Woodley RG5 21 F3
Church St, Caversham RG4 10 D6
Church St, Reading RG1 3 D4
Churchill Cl RG2 23 F1
Churchill Dr RG41 25 H3
Churchward Walk RG31 17 E5
Cinnamon Cl RG6 23 H3
Cintra Av RG2 19 F6
Circuit La RG30 17 G3
City Rd RG31 16 A2
Clanfield Cres RG31 8 B4
Clarence Way RG31 16 A4
Clarendon Cl RG41 26 B2
Clarendon Rd RG6 20 A5
Clares Green Rd RG7 28 D4
Clay Cl RG31 8 A3
Claydon Ct RG4 18 D1
Clayton Walk RG2 23 F1
Clements Cl RG7 28 D6
Clements Mead RG31 8 B6
Clent Rd RG2 19 E6
Clevedon Dr RG6 24 B3
Clevedon Rd RG31 8 D3
Cleveland Rd RG10 13 H4
Clifton Park Rd RG4 10 C6
Clifton Rd RG41 26 E4
Clifton St RG1 3 A3
Clivedale Rd RG5 21 E6
Clove Cl RG6 23 H4
Coalport Way RG30 9 E6
Cobham Dr RG5 21 F4
Cockney Hill RG30 17 E3
Cody Cl RG5 21 G2
Coldicutt St RG4 19 E1
Colemans Moor La RG5 21 F5

Colemans Moor Rd RG5 21 F
Coley Av RG1 3 A
Coley Hill RG1 3 A
Coley Park Rd RG1 18 C
Coley Pl RG1 3 B
College Rd RG6 19 H
Colliers Way RG30 17 G
Collingwood Walk RG31 16 A
Collis St RG2 18 E
Colliston Walk RG31 17 E
Colmworth Cl RG6 24 A
Colston Cl RG31 16
Colyton Way RG8 8
Combe Rd RG30 17
Comet Way RG5 21 C
Commercial Rd RG2 22
Commons Rd RG41 26
Compton Av RG31 16
Compton Cl RG6 20
Concorde Way RG5 21
Condor Cl RG31 8
Conifer Dr RG31 8
Conisboro Av RG4 10
Conisboro Way RG4 10
Coniston Cl RG5 21
Coniston Dr RG30 9
Connaught Cl RG30 18
Connaught Rd RG30 18
Conningham Rd RG2 23
Constable Cl RG5 21
Constitution Rd RG30 9
Consul Cl RG5 2
Conway Rd RG31 16
Conygree Cl RG6 24
Cooper Cl RG2 2
Copenhagen Cl RG2 2
Copperdale Cl RG6 23
Coppice Rd RG5 2
Copse Av RG4 11
Copse Cl RG31
Copse Mead RG5 2
Corbett Gdns RG5 2
Corbridge Rd RG2 2
Corby Cl RG5 2
Corfe Mews RG4 1
Corfield Grn RG41 2
Coriander Way RG6 2
Corinne Cl RG2 2
Cornfield Rd RG5 2
Cornwall Cl RG1
Cornwood Gdns RG2 2
Coronation Sq RG30 1
Corsham Rd RG31
Corwen Rd RG30 1
Cotswold Way RG31
Cottage La RG30
Cottesmore Rd RG5 2
Courage Ct RG30
Courtenay Dr RG4
Courts Rd RG6
Coventry Rd RG1
Cow La RG1
Cowper Way RG30
Cowslip Cl RG31
Craddock Rd RG2
Craig Av RG30
Cranbourne Av RG31
Cranbourne Gdns RG30
Cranbury Rd RG30
Crane Wharf RG1
Cranmer Cl RG4
Craven Rd RG1
Crawford Cl RG5
Crawshay Dr RG4
Crediton Cl RG5
Cremyll Rd RG1
Crendon Cl RG1
Crescent Rd, Reading RG1

rescent Rd,		Diana Cl RG7	28 D6	Edgar Milward Cl		Fairsted Cl RG30	9 E6	Foxes Walk RG10	13 G5
Tilehurst RG31	8 C6	Dickens Cl RG4	19 F1	RG30	9 F6	Fairview Av RG6	20 B5	*Foxglove Gdns,	
ressingham Rd RG2	23 E2	Doddington Cl RG6	24 C4	Edgehill St RG1	18 D6	Fairwater Dr RG5	20 C4	Stanley Gro RG1	18 B3
resswell Rd RG2	23 E6	Dolphin Cl RG41	26 A4	Edinburgh Rd RG30	18 A3	Fairway Av RG30	16 C2	Foxhays Rd RG2	23 F5
rispin Cl RG4	10 A3	Don Cl RG30	9 F6	Edward Rd RG10	13 H3	Fairway Dr RG10	13 G4	Foxhill Cl RG4	12 A4
rockhamwell Rd		Donaldson Way RG5	21 G3	Egerton Rd RG2	23 G4	Fakenham Cl RG6	24 A5	Foxhill La RG4	11 F1
RG5	21 E4	Donegal Cl RG4	11 E6	Egremont Dr RG6	24 D2	Falcon Av RG2	23 H4	Foxhill Rd RG1	19 G5
roft Rd RG2	29 E4	Donkin Hill RG4	11 F6	Elan Cl RG30	17 E2	Falkland Rd RG4	10 D6	Foxhunt Gro RG31	17 E5
romer Cl RG31	8 B6	Donnington Gdns		Eldart Cl RG30	17 G1	Fallowfield Cl RG4	11 E4	Framlingham Dr RG4	11 G3
romwell Rd RG4	11 E6	RG1	19 G4	Elder Cl RG31	8 B5	Falmouth Rd RG2	23 F6	Frampton Cl RG5	21 E2
oss St RG1	3 C3	Donnington Pl RG41	26 B3	Elderberry Way RG6	24 D3	Falstaff Av RG6	23 H2	Francis St RG1	18 D5
ossfields Cl RG2	23 G5	Donnington Rd RG1	19 G4	Eldon Pl RG1	3 F4	Faringdon Walk		Franklin St RG1	3 A3
ossland Rd RG1	3 D4	Dorchester Ct RG30	17 H3	Eldon Rd RG1	3 F3	RG30	17 G4	Fraser Av RG4	11 F2
ossways RG5	21 E6	Dorking Way RG31	16 A5	Eldon Sq RG1	3 F4	Farleigh Mews RG4	11 G3	Fraser Cl RG1	18 C1
own Pl RG1	3 E4	Dorothy St RG1	18 D4	Eldon St RG1	3 F3	Farm Cl RG8	8 B1	French Mews RG41	25 F1
own St RG1	3 D4	Dorset St RG30	9 H6	Eldon Ter RG1	3 F3	Farm Dr RG31	16 A2	Frensham Grn RG2	23 H4
ilford Cl RG4	24 D3	Douglas Grange		Elford Cl RG6	24 C3	Farman Cl RG5	21 H2	Freshfield Cl RG6	25 E1
ilver La RG6	20 A4	RG10	26 B1	Elgar Rd RG2	18 D5	Farmers Cl RG2	29 E1	Freshwater Rd RG1	19 G3
ilver Rd RG6	19 H4	Douglas Rd RG4	11 F6	Elgar Rd South RG2	18 D6	Farmers End RG10	13 H5	Friar St RG1	3 B2
mberland Rd RG1	19 G3	Dove Cl RG6	23 H5	Eliot Cl RG4	19 F1	Farmiloe Cl RG8	8 B2	Friars Walk RG1	3 C2
rlew Dr RG31	16 B2	Dovecote Rd RG2	23 E6	Elizabeth Ct RG31	8 C6	Farnham Dr RG4	11 G4	Frieth Cl RG6	24 A3
rtis Rd RG31	16 B4	Dovedale Cl RG4	10 C6	Elizabeth Rout Cl		Farnsfield Cl RG6	24 A5	Frilsham Rd RG30	17 G4
rzon St RG30	18 A3	Dover St RG1	18 C4	RG7	29 E5	Farriers Cl RG5	21 E3	Frimley Cl RG5	20 D2
tbush Cl RG6	24 B4	Dowding Cl RG5	21 G4	Elizabeth Walk RG2	19 E5	Farrowdene Rd RG2	23 E5	Fringford Cl RG6	24 C4
tbush La,		Downing Rd RG31	8 C6	Ellesmere Cl RG4	11 E5	Fatherson Rd RG1	19 F3	Frogmore Way RG30	17 G4
ower Earley RG6	24 C4	Downs Way RG31	8 B4	Elliots Way RG1	18 D1	Fawcett Cres RG5	20 D4	Froxfield Av RG1	18 B5
tbush La,		Downshire Sq RG1	18 B4	Elm La RG6	23 H2	Fawley Rd RG30	17 H3	Fuchsia Cl RG31	16 B3
ower Earley RG6	24 B5	Drayton Rd RG30	9 G6	Elm Lodge Av RG30	17 H1	Faygate Way RG6	24 B4	Fulbrook Cres RG31	8 C3
tbush La,		Dresden Way RG30	9 E6	Elm Park Ct RG30	17 H2	Felixstowe Cl RG6	24 D3	Fulham Rd RG1	18 D5
shinfield RG2	24 A6	Drewett Cl RG2	23 F6	Elm Park Rd RG30	18 A4	Felstead Cl RG6	23 H2	Fullbrook Cl RG41	26 E4
ncarn Rd RG4	10 C3	Driftway Cl RG6	24 D4	Elm Rd, Earley RG6	23 H3	Felthorpe Cl RG6	24 A5	Fullers La RG7	28 A3
ress Rd RG5	21 G5	Drome Path RG41	25 G2	Elm Rd,		Felton Way RG31	8 B6	Fulmead Rd RG30	9 H6
		Drovers Way RG5	21 E5	Tokers Green RG4	10 A1	Fennel Cl RG6	24 A4	Fulmer Cl RG6	24 A3
re Av RG4	11 G4	Dudley Cl RG31	8 D5	Elmhurst Rd RG1	19 F6	Fern Cl RG31	16 B3		
e Rd RG2	18 D5	Dudley Mews RG31	8 D5	Elmleigh Ct RG4	11 F6	Fern Glen RG31	8 B5	Gainsborough Cl	
on Cl RG30	16 D1	Duffield Rd RG5	21 E1	Elmley Cl RG41	26 D4	Fern Walk RG31	16 C4	RG5	21 G4
ehill RG6	23 H2	Duke St RG1	3 D3	Elmstone Dr RG31	8 B5	Fernbrook Dr RG4	10 A4	Gainsborough Rd	
ywern Dr RG41	26 A2	Dulnan Cl RG30	9 F6	Elsley Rd RG31	8 C4	Ferndale Av RG30	17 F4	RG30	17 F4
ell Rd RG4	10 B5	Dulverton Gdns RG2	23 F3	Elstow Av RG4	11 F2	Ferndale Cl RG31	8 D3	Gairn Cl RG30	17 F1
k La RG31	8 A5	Dunaways Cl RG6	24 D1	Elstree Cl RG31	8 C4	Fernhurst Rd RG31	16 B5	Galsworthy Dr RG4	11 G3
ington Av RG5	20 D6	Dunbar Dr RG5	21 G4	Eltham Av RG4	11 G3	Field Rd RG1	3 B4	Garde Rd RG4	13 E5
ington Cl RG30	9 E6	Dunbarton Way RG4	11 G3	Elvaston Way RG30	17 E1	Field Vw RG4	11 E5	Garnet Hill RG1	3 B4
mouth Ter RG1	1 D4	Duncan Gdns RG8	8 B2	Elvedon Cl RG6	25 E3	Fieldway RG41	26 B2	Garnet St RG1	18 C4
vin Cl RG2	22 D3	Duncan Rd RG5	21 E4	Elyham RG8	8 B2	Filbert Dr RG31	8 B6	Garrard St RG1	3 B2
s Cl RG4	25 H3	Dundela Cl RG5	21 E5	Embrook Ct RG6	23 H3	Filey Rd RG1	19 G3	Garston Cl RG30	17 F4
s St RG10	26 B1	Dunholme Cl RG6	25 E2	Embrook Way RG31	16 A5	Finback Way RG6	24 A5	Garston Cres RG31	16 B4
s Way RG10	26 B1	Dunoon Cl RG31	16 D5	Emm Cl RG41	26 D4	Finch Rd RG6	24 C1	Garth Cl RG41	26 A3
ish Rd RG2	23 E2	Dunsfold Rd RG30	17 E2	Emmbrook Gate		Finstock Cl RG6	24 D4	Gas Works Rd RG1	3 F3
eauvoir Rd RG1	19 G4	Dunstall Cl RG31	8 C6	RG41	26 D4	Fircroft Cl RG31	8 B5	Gaskells End RG4	10 A1
ohun Rd RG1	3 D1	Dunstans Dr RG41	25 G3	Emmbrook Rd RG41	26 D4	Firmstone Cl RG6	24 C4	Gatcombe Cl RG31	16 B4
ontfort Rd RG1	3 C1	Dunster Cl RG4	11 F2	Emmbrook Vale		Firs La RG30	18 A6	Gayhurst Cl RG4	11 F2
on Way RG30	9 F5	Dunt Av RG10	26 C1	RG41	26 E4	Firs Rd RG30	16 B3	Gazelle Cl RG41	25 F1
s Farm RG4	19 F1	Dunt La RG10	26 C1	Emmer Green Ct RG4	11 E3	Fishers Ct RG6	11 E2	Gelder Cl RG6	24 D4
sgate Rd RG1	3 C4	Durand Rd RG6	24 A4	Empress Rd RG31	16 C4	Fitzroy Cres RG5	21 F4	Geoffreyson Rd RG4	10 A3
Rd RG30	17 E2	Durham Cl RG2	23 F4	Enborne Ct RG31	16 C1	Five Acre RG6	8 B6	George St RG1	3 D1
dene Cl RG1	18 B4	Durrant Way RG31	8 C3	Ennerdale Rd RG2	23 F1	Flambards RG4	11 F6	Gifford Cl RG4	11 G3
hurst Av RG41	24 A2	Dusseldorf Way RG1	3 B3	Enstone Rd RG5	21 G3	Flamborough Cl RG6	25 E3	Gillette Way RG2	22 D2
hurst Cl RG31	16 A2	Dwyer Rd RG30	17 F4	Epping Cl RG1	3 A4	*Flamborough Path,		Gingells Farm Rd	
rd Cl RG41	26 D6			Epsom Ct RG1	18 B5	Flamborough Cl		RG10	13 G4
eld Dr RG31	16 B5	Earley Hill Rd RG6	20 A6	Eric Av RG4	10 D2	RG6	25 E3	Gipsy La, Earley RG6	24 C3
here Rd RG6	20 B3	Earley Pl RG1	3 C3	Eriswell Cl RG6	25 E3	Flaxman Cl RG6	23 H3	Gipsy La, Earley RG6	24 D2
e Dr RG41	25 H3	Earlsfield Cl RG4	11 G4	Erleigh Court Dr RG6	20 B3	Fleetham Gdns RG6	24 C3	Gipsy La,	
ey Cl RG30	9 E6	Easby Way RG6	24 D3	Erleigh Court Gdns		Flodden Dr RG31	16 C4	Sindlesham RG41	25 F5
Cl RG30	9 E6	Easington Dr RG6	25 E3	RG6	20 A3	Florence Ct RG30	18 A5	Gipsy La,	
d RG31	8 B5	East Dr RG30,31	16 D3	Erleigh Rd RG1	3 F4	Florence Walk RG1	19 G3	Tilehurst RG30	8 D5
eigh Pl RG1	18 C1	East Park Farm Dr		Eskdale Rd RG41	25 G1	Florian Gdns RG30	17 G3	Gladridge Cl RG6	20 C6
ury Gdns RG2	23 E4	RG10	13 G5	Eskin Cl RG30	17 F1	Florida Ct RG1	18 B4	Glamis Way RG31	16 A4
Way RG30	9 E6	East St RG1	3 D3	Essex St RG2	19 E6	Fobney St RG1	3 C4	Glebe Gdns RG4	13 E5
Cl RG6	24 B2	Eastbury Av RG31	16 B1	Evergreen Dr RG31	17 E4	Fontwell Dr RG30	17 E3	Glebe La RG4	13 E6
ark Av RG5	21 F1	Eastbury Pk RG4	26 B3	Evesham Rd RG4	10 D3	Forbury Rd RG1	3 D2	Glebe Rd,	
ark Rd RG1	19 F4	Eastcourt Av RG6	20 A4	Exbourne Rd RG6	23 E5	Fordham Way RG6	24 C4	Purley on Thames	
se Cl RG6	24 B3	Eastern Av RG1	19 G4	Exeter Ct RG2	23 E5	Forest Dean RG2	23 E6	RG8	8 A1
Rd RG4	11 E5	Eastwood Ct RG5	21 E6	Exwick Sq RG2	23 F4	Forest Hill RG30	9 E5	Glebe Rd,	
St RG1	18 B3	Eastwood Rd RG5	21 E6	Eynsford Cl RG4	11 G3	Forest Rd RG40	26 F2	Reading RG2	19 E6
k Cl RG31	16 B4	Eaton Pl RG1	3 A3	Eynsham Cl RG5	21 E2	Forge Cl RG4	19 F1	Glemsford Cl RG6	25 E2
nt Av RG30	8 D4	Ebborn Sq RG6	24 C4			Formby Cl RG6	25 E1	Glenbeigh Ter RG1	18 B4
on Dr RG30	9 F6	Eccles Cl RG4	11 F6	Faircross Rd RG30	17 H4	Fordon Cl RG6	25 E3	Glendevon Rd RG5	21 F2
Cl RG6	23 H3	Eden Way RG41	25 H3	Fairfax Cl RG4	11 E6	Fortrose Walk RG31	17 E5	Glennon Cl RG30	17 H4
Dr RG4	11 H4	Edenhall Cl RG31	16 B4	Fairford Rd RG31	8 B5	Fosters La RG5	21 E5	Glenrhondda RG4	10 C3
shire Gdns		Edenham Cl RG6	25 E3	Fairlawn Grn RG2	23 H3	Foundry Pl RG1	3 C4	Glenrosa Rd RG30	9 F6
1	8 B3	Edenham Cres RG1	18 A6	Fairlop Cl RG31	16 C5	Fowler Cl RG6	24 A2	Glenwood Dr RG31	16 B2
shire Pk RG6	23 H2			Fairmead Rd RG2	29 H2	Foxcombe Dr RG31	16 B1	Gloucester Ct RG30	18 A4

Gloucester Rd RG30 18 A4
Glyme Walk RG31 17 E5
Glyncastle RG4 10 B3
Goddard Cl RG2 29 H1
Goddard Ct RG41 25 H3
Godstow Rd RG5 21 E2
Goldcrest Way RG31 16 B2
Goldsmid Rd RG1 3 A3
Goldthorpe Gdns
  RG6 23 H5
Goodliffe Gdns RG31 8 B3
Goodrich Cl RG4 11 G3
Goodwin Rd RG31 16 D5
*Gordon Palmer Ct,
  Oxford Rd RG30 9 H6
Gordon Pl RG30 9 H6
Gorse Dr RG5 21 G3
Gorselands RG4 10 D2
Gosbrook Rd RG4 19 E1
Gosforth Cl RG6 24 D2
Gower St RG1 18 B3
Graffham Cl RG6 24 B4
Grafton Rd RG30 16 C1
Graham Cl RG31 16 D4
Granby Ct RG1 19 G4
Granby Gdns RG1 19 G4
Grange Av RG6 20 A4
Grangely Cl RG31 16 C4
Grantham Rd RG30 17 E5
Granville Rd RG30 17 F4
Grasmere Av RG30 9 E4
Grasmere Cl RG41 25 H4
Grass Hill RG4 10 B6
Gratton Rd RG2 23 F5
Gratwicke Rd RG30 16 D1
Gravel Hill RG4 10 B2
Graveney Dr RG4 10 B5
Grays Cres RG5 20 C3
Grazeley Rd RG7 28 C3
Great Knollys St RG1 3 A2
Great Lea Ter RG7 28 D1
Green La,
  Hurst RG10 26 C1
Green La,
  Winnersh RG41 26 B4
Green Rd RG6 20 A5
Greenacre Mount
  RG30 8 D6
Greenacres Av RG41 25 G2
Greenacres La RG41 25 G2
Greencroft Gdns
  RG30 17 E4
Greenend RG7 29 E4
Greenfields Rd RG2 23 E5
Greenfinch Cl RG31 16 B2
Greenham Cl RG5 21 G5
Greenidge Cl RG1 18 A5
Greenleas Av RG4 11 E1
Greenwood RG41 26 B2
Greenwood Rd RG30 17 E4
Gregory Cl RG6 24 C5
Gresham Way RG30 9 F4
Greyfriars Rd RG1 3 B2
Greys Ct RG1 3 E4
Greystoke Rd RG4 11 E5
Grosvenor Rd RG4 11 E5
Grove Cotts RG4 10 D3
Grove Hill RG4 10 D4
Grove Rd RG4 10 D3
Groveland Pl RG30 9 G6
Grovelands Av RG41 26 B2
Grovelands Cl RG41 26 B2
Grovelands Rd,
  Spencers Wood
  RG7 29 E5
Grovelands Rd,
  Tilehurst RG30 9 G6
Gun St RG1 3 C3
Gurney Cl RG4 10 A4
Gurney Dr RG4 10 A4
Gwynne Cl RG31 8 C3

Hackfield Dr RG41 26 B4
Haddon Dr RG5 21 E2
Hadleigh Rise RG4 11 G3
Hadrian Walk East
  RG2 23 F1
Hadrian Walk West
  RG2 23 F1
Hafod RG4 10 C2
Hagley Rd RG2 19 E6
Halcyon Ter RG30 8 D6
Haldane Rd RG4 10 B4
Halds La RG2 23 H4
Halls Rd RG30 16 B2
Halpin Cl RG31 16 B4
Halstead Cl RG5 21 E3
Hamble Ct RG1 3 C4
Hambleberry Ct RG31 8 C6
Hambledon Cl RG6 25 E3
Hamilton Rd RG1 19 G4
Hampden Rd RG4 11 E6
Hanbury Dr RG31 16 C4
Hanover Ct RG4 11 E3
Hanwood Cl RG5 20 C2
Harcourt Dr RG6 23 H2
Harding Rd RG5 21 F1
Hardwick Rd RG30 17 E1
Hardy Cl RG4 11 E6
Harefield Cl RG41 26 B2
Hargreaves Way
  RG31 17 E4
Harlech Av RG4 11 G3
Harley Rd RG4 18 D1
Harlton Cl RG6 24 C5
Harman Ct RG41 25 H3
Harness Cl RG2 23 E6
Harrier Cl RG5 21 G4
Harrington Cl RG6 24 C2
Harris Arcade RG1 3 C2
Harris Cl RG5 21 H2
Harrogate Rd RG4 10 B5
Harrow Ct RG1 18 B4
Harry Tee Ct RG1 3 F3
Hart St RG1 18 B3
Hartigan Pl RG5 21 G3
Hartland Rd RG2 23 E4
Hartsbourne Rd RG6 24 A1
Hartslock Way RG31 8 C5
Harvard Cl RG5 21 G2
Harvaston Par RG30 17 E1
Harvest RG31 16 A2
Harwich Cl RG6 24 D5
Hastings Rd RG30 17 F5
Hatchway RG2 23 F6
Hatfield Ct RG31 16 A5
Hatford Rd RG30 17 F4
Hatherley Rd RG1 19 G4
Haven Ct RG1 19 G3
Hawkchurch Rd RG2 23 F4
Hawkedon Way RG6 24 D3
Hawker Way RG5 21 G4
Hawkesbury Dr RG31 16 D5
Hawley Cl RG31 16 C4
Hawthorn Gdns RG2 23 G2
Hawthorn Way RG4 13 E6
Hawthorne Rd RG4 11 G5
Hawthornes RG31 8 B4
Hay Rd RG1 18 C6
Hayfield Cl RG31 8 B6
Haywood Ct RG1 19 H3
Haywood Way RG30 17 E3
Hazel Cres RG2 23 G2
Hazel Dr RG5 20 C6
Hazel Rd RG8 8 B2
Hazelwood Cl RG31 8 B6
Heacham Cl RG6 24 A5
Headley Cl RG5 21 G3
Headley Rd RG5 21 E3
Headley Rd East RG5 21 F3
Hearn Rd RG5 21 E5

Heath Rd RG6 20 A6
Heatherden Cl RG2 23 E5
Heathfield Rd RG30 16 C2
Heathway RG31 16 B1
Helen Ct RG30 17 F4
Helmsdale Cl RG30 17 G1
Helston Gdns RG2 23 E3
Hemdean Hill RG4 10 D6
Hemdean Rd RG4 10 D6
Hemdean Rise RG4 10 D6
Hengrave Cl RG6 25 E3
Henley Rd RG4 11 E6
Henley Wood Rd
  RG6 24 D1
Henry St RG1 3 C4
Herald Way RG5 21 G4
Heroes Walk RG2 23 E6
Heron Island RG4 19 E1
Heron Way RG1 18 B6
Hertford Cl RG4 11 F3
Hewett Av RG4 10 A5
Hewett Cl RG4 10 A4
Hexham Rd RG2 23 E1
High Mdw RG4 10 A5
High St, Reading RG1 3 D3
High St,
  Sonning RG4 12 D5
High Tree Dr RG5 20 B4
Highbridge Cl RG4 11 G4
Highbridge Wharf
  RG1 3 D3
Highbury Rd RG31 16 A2
Highcliffe Cl RG5 21 F1
Highdown Av RG4 10 C2
Highdown Hill Rd
  RG4 10 C2
Highfield Rd RG31 8 B2
Highfields RG6 24 B2
Highgate Rd RG5 20 D5
Highgrove St RG1 19 E5
Highgrove Ter RG1 19 E5
Highmead Cl RG2 23 G2
Highmoor Rd RG4 10 B5
Highview RG31 16 A4
Highworth Way RG31 8 A5
Hilary Cl RG2 23 F5
Hilbury Rd RG6 24 A2
Hilcot Rd RG30 18 A3
Hildens Dr RG31 16 B2
Hill St RG1 18 D5
Hillbrow RG2 23 G3
Hillside RG1 19 F5
Hillside Pk RG2 23 H3
Hillside Rd RG6 24 D2
Hilltop Rd,
  Caversham RG4 10 A3
Hilltop Rd,
  Earley RG6 20 B3
Hillview Cl RG31 8 A4
Hilmanton RG6 23 H4
Hindhead Rd RG6 24 A2
Hirstwood RG30 8 D5
Hirtes Av RG2 29 H2
Hodsoll Rd RG1 3 A2
Hogarth Av RG30 17 E3
Holberton Rd RG2 23 F4
Holford Cl RG31 8 B6
Holkham Cl RG30 9 E6
Holland Rd RG30 16 C2
Hollicombe Cl RG30 16 B1
Hollins Walk RG30 17 H2
Hollow La RG2 29 G1
Holly Rd RG5 21 G5
Hollydale Cl RG2 23 G4
Hollym Cl RG6 25 E3
Holme Park Farm La
  RG4 20 C1
Holmemoor Dr RG4 20 D1
Holmes Rd RG6 20 A6
Holmwood Av RG30 17 E4
Holsworthy Cl RG6 25 E2
Holybrook Cres RG30 17 F4

Holybrook Rd RG1 18 C5
Holymead RG31 17 E4
Holyrood Cl RG4 11 F2
Home Cft RG31 8 B6
Home Farm Cl RG2 23 E1
Honey End La RG30 17 F2
Honey Meadow Cl
  RG4 11 G6
Honiton Rd RG2 23 E3
Hoops Way RG2 29 H2
Hornbeam Cl RG8 8 B2
Hornbeam Dr RG6 24 D3
Horncastle Dr RG30 17 E4
Hornsea Cl RG30 8 D6
Hosier St RG1 3 C3
Howard St RG1 3 B3
Howth Dr RG5 20 D3
Huckleberry Cl RG8 8 B2
Hudson Rd RG5 21 F5
Hugh Fraser Dr RG30 16 C2
Hungerford Dr RG1 18 B5
Hunters Chase RG4 10 B3
Hunters Way RG7 28 D5
Huntingdon Cl RG6 25 E2
Huntley Ct RG1 19 G4
Hurricane Way RG5 21 G3
Hursley Cl RG30 16 D1
Hurst Way RG2 22 C5
Huscarle Way RG31 8 B2
Hutton Cl RG6 24 A3
Hyde End La RG7 29 E2
Hyde End Rd RG7 28 D5
Hyperion Way RG2 22 D1

Ian Mikardo Way
  RG4 11 G6
Ibstock Cl RG30 17 G1
Ibstone Av RG4 11 G3
Ilbury Cl RG2 29 G2
Ilfracombe Way RG6 25 E2
Ilkley Rd RG4 10 B5
*Illchester Mews,
  Illingworth Av RG4 11 G3
Illingworth Av RG4 11 G3
Imperial Way RG2 22 D5

INDUSTRIAL & RETAIL:
Acre Rd Business Pk
  RG2 22 D4
Broad St Mall RG1 3 B3
Brunel Retail Pk
  RG2 22 D2
Cardiff Rd Industrial Est
  RG1 3 A1
Forbury Industrial Est
  RG1 3 F2
*Gresham Way Industrial
  Est, Gresham Way
  RG30 9 F4
Headley Pk Industrial Est
  RG5 21 F3
Kidbys Industrial Est
  RG1 18 C5
Meadway Precinct
  RG30 17 F2
Oxford Rd Industrial Est
  RG30 9 E4
Paddock Rd Industrial Est
  RG4 19 F1
Reading Gate Retail Pk
  RG2 22 C4
Reading Link Business Pk
  RG1 18 C6
Reading Retail Pk
  RG30 9 G6
Stadium Way
  Industrial Est RG30 9 G5
Suttons Business Pk
  RG4 19 H2
Suttons Industrial Pk
  RG6 20 A3

Thames Valley Business
Pk
  RG6 20 A
The Oracle
  Shopping Centre
  RG1 3 C
Winnersh Triangle
  Industrial Est
  RG41 25 G
Woodside Business Pk
  RG2 23 B
Worton Grange
  Industrial Est RG2 22 D

Inglewood Ct RG30 17 F
Inkpen Cl RG30 17
Instow Rd RG6 24
Invergordon Cl RG31 17 F
Irvine Way RG6 24
Isis Cl RG41 25
Isis Ct RG1 3
Island Rd RG2 22
Ivybank RG31 8
Ivydene Rd RG30 9

Jacksons La RG4 9
James St RG1 18
Janson Ct RG1 3
Jay Cl RG6 24
Jefferson Cl RG4 11
Jenkins Cl RG30 17
Jerome Rd RG5 20
Jesse Ter RG1 3
Joel Cl RG6 24
Johannes Ct RG30 18
Jordan Cl,
  Caversham RG4 11
Jordon Cl,
  Spencers Wood
  RG7 2
Josephine Ct RG30 18
Jubilee Rd RG6 2
Jubilee Sq RG1 3
Julkes La RG2 2
Junction Rd RG1 19
Juniper Way RG31

Katesgrove La RG1
Keane Cl RG5 2
Kearsley Rd RG30
Keats Cl RG5 2
Keats Rd RG5 2
Kelburne Cl RG41 2
Kelmscott Cl RG4
Kelso Mews RG4 1
Kelton Cl RG6
Kelvedon Way RG4 1
Kemble Ct RG31
Kemerton Cl RG31
Kenavon Dr RG1
Kendal Av,
  Caversham RG4
Kendal Av,
  Shinfield RG2
Kendrick Rd RG1
Kenilworth Av RG30
Kennedy Gdns RG6
Kennet Side RG1
Kennet St RG1
Kensington Cl RG6
Kensington Rd RG30
Kent Rd RG30
Kentford Cl RG6
Kenton Rd RG6
Kentwood Cl RG30
Kentwood Hill RG31
Kernham Dr RG31
Kerris Way RG6
Keston Cl RG4
Kestrel Way RG30
Keswick Cl RG30
Keswick Gdns RG5

Lettering Cl RG31 16 D4
...idmore End Rd RG4 10 C1
...idmore Rd RG4 10 B2
...ilburn Cl RG31 16 C4
...ildare Gdns RG4 11 F5
...iln La RG31 8 A6
...iln Rd RG4 11 F2
...In View Rd RG2 23 F2
...insea Dr RG6 24 D2
...lowna Cl RG10 13 G4
...mberley Cl RG1 18 A5
...mpton Cl RG6 23 H5
...ng St RG1 3 D3
...ng Street La RG41 25 G5
...ngfisher Dr RG5 20 C4
...ngfisher Pl RG1 3 D1
...ngs Meadow Rd RG1 3 D1
...ngs Rd, Caversham RG4 19 E1
...ngs Rd, Reading RG1 3 D3
...gs Walk RG1 1 D3
...gsbridge Rd RG2 23 E2
...gsford Cl RG5 21 G5
...ngsgate Pl, Kingsbury St RG1 19 G3
...gsgate St RG1 19 G3
...gsley Cl, Charvil RG10 13 G3
...gsley Cl, Reading RG2 22 D6
...gston Gdns RG2 23 E2
...gsway RG4 11 G3
...gswood Ct RG30 18 A4
...son Rd RG30 9 F5
...bury Walk RG30 17 H4
...ling Cl, ...ivedale Rd RG5 21 E6
...fell Cl RG31 8 B5
...ham La RG4 11 G3
...stall Ct RG31 16 C4
...on Cl RG30 17 G1
...wake Cl RG5 21 H4
...ood Dr RG6 25 E3
...hton Cl RG4 10 D5
...hts Way RG4 11 E3
...er Walk RG2 19 E5
...mead RG31 16 C4
...sington Cl RG6 24 C3
...le Cl RG4 10 A4
...le Rd RG5 21 E6
...sley Rd RG3 8 A3
...s La RG7 28 A2

...rnum Gdns ...2 23 G3
...num Rd RG41 26 A4
...wood Gdns RG2 23 G4
...oke Cl RG5 21 F4
...Jane Ct RG4 11 E5
...mask Cl RG31 17 E4
...ide RG6 24 B2
...eth Ct RG30 17 E2
...ourn Cl RG31 8 C6
...ourne Gdns
...s 20 D6
...wood Hill RG7 28 A5
...ton Rd RG2 23 E4
...na Cres RG31 8 B5
...lighters Walk, ...ymask Cl RG31 17 E4
...Cl RG5 21 G4
...ster Cl RG1 19 F5
...ster Gdns RG6 24 B1
...g Cl RG30 18 A4
...ke Cres RG2 23 E3
...nd La RG10 13 H6
...nd Cl RG2 29 G1
...le Gdns RG6 23 H3
...rd Cl RG4 11 E3

Langley Hill RG31 16 B3
Langley Hill Cl RG31 16 B3
Langley La RG2 24 D6
Laniver Ct RG6 24 D6
Lansdowne Gdns RG7 29 F5
Lansdowne Rd RG30 16 C2
Lapwing Cl RG31 16 B3
Larch Dr RG5 21 E6
Larchside RG7 28 D5
Larissa Cl RG31 8 D5
Larks Meade RG6 24 A3
Larkswood Cl RG31 8 B6
Latimer Dr RG31 16 B5
Laud Cl RG1 18 D5
Launceston Av RG4 11 G3
Launceston Cl RG6 24 B2
Laurel Dr RG31 8 B6
Lavenham Dr RG5 21 F2
Lavenheath Cl RG6 25 E2
Lawrence Rd RG30 9 F6
Lawson Dr RG4 10 B4
Layton Rise RG31 8 A4
Lea Cl RG30 17 F5
Leander Pl RG31 16 D5
Ledbury Cl RG30 9 G6
Ledbury Dr RG31 16 C5
Ledran Cl RG6 24 C4
Leighton Ct RG6 23 H1
Leiston Cl RG6 24 D3
Lemart Cl RG30 8 D6
Lenham Cl RG41 26 C4
Lennox Cl RG31 16 B5
Lennox Rd RG6 20 A5
Leopold Walk RG1 19 F3
Lesford Rd RG1 18 B6
Lesley Cl RG30 18 A4
Letcombe St RG1 3 D4
Lexington Gro RG2 23 E6
Leyburn Cl RG5 21 G2
Leyland Gdns RG2 29 G1
Lichfield Cl RG6 24 C3
Lidstone Cl RG6 24 D1
Liebenrood Rd RG30 17 H2
Lilac Cl RG8 8 C2
Lilac Walk RG31 16 B3
Lima Ct RG1 3 A4
Limefield Cl RG6 25 E1
Lincoln Cl RG41 25 G2
Lincoln Rd RG2 23 E1
Lind Cl RG4 24 C2
Lindberg Way RG5 21 H2
Linden Rd, Reading RG2 23 G3
Linden Rd, Woodley RG5 20 D6
Linear Way RG31 16 B5
Lingholm Cl RG30 17 E3
Links Dr RG30 9 F5
Linnet Cl RG31 16 A2
Lismore Cl RG5 21 E6
Lister Cl RG8 8 B1
Littington Cl RG6 24 C4
Little Glebe RG4 13 E6
Little Heath Rd RG31 8 A6
Little Hill Rd RG10 26 B1
Little Johns La RG30 9 H6
Little Oaks Dr RG31 8 B6
Little St RG1 18 B3
Littlecote Dr RG1 18 B5
Littlestead Cl RG4 11 H3
Litton Rd RG2 23 F3
Liverpool Rd RG1 19 G3
Livery Cl RG1 3 E4
Livingstone Gdns RG5 21 E5
Loaders La RG2 25 E6
Lock Pl RG1 19 F3
Loddon Bridge Rd RG5,6 21 F3
Loddon Dr RG10 13 G1
Logan Cl RG30 17 E1

Lomond Av RG4 11 G3
London Rd, Reading RG1 3 D4
London Rd, Woodley RG6 20 A3
London St RG1 3 D3
Long Barn La RG2 23 E1
Long La RG31 8 A3
Longdon Rd RG41 25 H4
Longhurst RG4 11 F5
Longleat Dr RG31 8 A4
Longmore Rd RG2 29 F1
Longridge RG20 17 G1
Longwater Av RG2 22 A4
Longworth Av RG31 16 A1
Lorne Pl RG2 23 F2
Lorne St RG1 18 B3
Lovatt Cl RG31 16 B1
Loverock Rd RG30 9 H5
Low La RG31 17 E4
Lower Armour Rd RG31 8 C5
Lower Brook St RG1 18 D4
Lower Earley Way RG6 23 G6
Lower Elmstone Dr RG31 8 B5
Lower Field Rd RG1 18 C4
Lower Henley Rd RG4 11 F6
Lower Meadow Rd RG2 23 F2
Lower Mount RG1 19 F5
Lowestoft Cl RG6 24 D3
Lowfield Grn RG4 11 G4
Lowfield Rd RG4 11 E3
Lowther Cl RG41 26 D4
Lowther Rd RG41 26 D4
Loxwood RG6 24 C3
Lucey Cl RG31 8 B4
Luckmore Dr RG6 24 A1
Lulworth Rd RG2 23 F5
Lunds Farm Rd RG5 21 F3
Lundy La RG30 17 H1
Luscombe Cl RG4 11 F6
Lutton Cl RG2 24 A5
Lydford Rd RG1 19 G5
Lyfield Ct RG4 11 E3
Lyme Gro RG31 8 C6
Lymington Gate RG4 10 B4
Lynden Mews RG2 18 D5
Lyndhurst Rd RG30 19 G2
Lynmouth Rd RG1 3 C1
Lynton Cl RG5 20 C5
Lyon Sq RG30 17 F1
Lysander Cl RG5 21 G3
Lytham Cl RG30 17 G4
Lytham End RG31 8 B3
Lytham Rd RG5 21 E3

Mace Cl RG6 24 A4
Mackay Cl RG31 16 D5
Magill Cl RG7 29 E5
Magnolia Ct RG5 21 G3
Magpie Way RG31 16 A3
Maiden Erlegh Dr RG6 20 B6
Maiden Pl RG6 24 D3
Maidensfield RG41 26 B2
Maitland Rd RG1 18 B4
Maiwand Gdns RG31 16 C2
Maker Cl RG30 17 G4
Maldon Cl RG5 18 A4
Mallard Cl RG6 24 A1
Mallard Row RG1 3 B4
Mallory Av RG4 11 F2
Malone Rd RG5 20 D5
Maltby Way RG2 24 A5
Malthouse Cl RG2 3 A2
Malthouse La RG1 3 A2
Maltings Pl RG1 3 C4
Malvern Cl RG5 21 E4
Malvern Ct RG1 19 G5

Managua Cl RG4 11 G6
Manchester Rd RG1 19 H3
Mandela Cl RG1 3 F3
Mander Ct RG4 11 E5
Mandeville Cl RG30 17 E3
Manea Cl RG6 24 C5
Manners Rd RG5 20 D3
Mannock Way RG5 21 G2
Manor Farm Rd RG2 22 D3
Manor House Ct RG6 20 A6
Manor Park Cl RG30 16 C2
Mansell Ct RG2 23 G2
Mansfield Rd RG1 18 C5
Maple Cl RG41 26 B1
Maple Gdns RG2 23 G2
Mapledene RG4 10 B5
Mapledurham Dr RG8 8 C1
Mapledurham Vw RG31 8 C4
Marathon Cl RG5 21 H2
Marchwood Av RG4 11 F1
Marcus Cl RG30 17 G2
Marefield Rd RG6 24 C2
Marfleet Cl RG6 25 E3
Margaret Cl RG2 23 E6
Maria Ct RG30 18 A4
Markby Way RG6 24 D2
Market Pl RG1 3 D3
Market Way RG1 3 D3
Marks Rd RG41 26 E4
Marlborough Av RG1 19 F6
Marlborough Ct RG1 18 B5
Marlborough Way RG31 16 A4
Marling Cl RG31 16 B5
Marquis Pl RG1 19 G4
Marsack St RG4 11 E6
Marsh Ct RG30 18 A3
Marsh La RG4 12 A4
Marshall Cl RG8 8 C2
Marshland Sq RG4 11 E4
Marten Pl RG31 8 B3
Martin Cl RG5 21 E5
Mason Ct RG1 18 B3
Mason St RG1 18 B3
Master Cl RG5 21 H2
Matlock Rd RG4 10 B5
Matthews Green Rd RG41 26 E4
Mawbray Cl RG6 24 C2
Maxwell Cl RG5 21 E2
May Pk RG31 17 E4
Mayfair RG30 16 C1
Mayfield Av RG31 16 A4
Mayfield Dr RG4 11 F5
Mayfields RG41 25 G4
Mays Cl RG6 20 B5
Mays La RG6 20 B5
McNair Cl RG6 24 A4
Mead Cl RG31 16 A2
Meadow Rd, Earley RG6 24 D1
Meadow Rd, Reading RG1 3 A1
Meadow Vw RG41 26 B1
Meadowcroft Rd RG2 23 E5
Meadowside RG31 8 A5
Measham Way RG6 24 C3
Meavy Gdns RG2 23 E3
Melbourne Av RG41 26 A3
Meldreth Way RG6 24 C4
Melford Grn RG4 11 G3
Melksham Cl RG3 23 H4
Melling Cl RG6 25 E2
Mellor Walk RG2 19 E6
Melody Cl RG4 11 G4
Melrose Av RG6 20 A6
Mendip Cl RG10 13 H4
*Mendip Dr, Stratford Way RG31 16 A2
Menpes Rd RG31 8 B3
Merchants Pl RG1 3 C2

Mereoak La RG7 28 B4
Mereoak Orch RG7 28 D1
Mereoak Pk RG7 28 D2
Mermaid Cl RG41 25 H3
Merrifield Cl RG6 24 D4
Merrivale Gdns RG2 23 E3
Merryhill Chase RG41 26 B1
Merryhill Green La RG41 26 B1
Merthyr Vale RG4 10 C2
Merton Rd North RG2 23 E3
Merton Rd South RG2 23 E4
Meteor Cl RG5 21 G4
Mey Cl RG31 16 C4
Micklands Rd RG4 11 G5
Microsoft Campus RG6 20 B2
Midsummer Mdw RG4 10 B3
Midwinter Cl RG30 8 D6
Mildenhall Cl RG6 24 D3
Miles Way RG5 21 G4
Milestone Av RG10 13 F2
Milestone Cres RG10 13 G4
Milestone Way RG4 11 F3
Milford Rd RG1 3 A1
Mill Grn RG4 19 E1
Mill La, Calcot RG31 16 D5
Mill La, Earley RG6 25 E1
Mill La, Earley RG6 25 E2
Mill La, Reading RG1 3 C4
Mill Rd RG4 19 E1
Millbank Cres RG5 21 F5
Millers Ct RG4 19 F1
Millers Gro RG31 17 E4
Millworth La RG2 29 H3
Milman Rd RG2 19 E6
Milsom Cl RG2 29 G1
Milton Rd RG6 20 A3
Minster St RG1 3 C3
Mint Cl RG6 24 A3
Minton Cl RG30 9 E6
Mitcham Cl RG2 19 E6
Mitchell Way RG5 21 G4
Mitford Cl RG2 23 G5
Modbury Gdns RG2 23 F2
Mohawk Way RG5 21 H2
Mole Rd RG41 25 F6
Mollison Cl RG5 21 H2
Monkley Ct RG4 19 F1
Monks Way RG30 18 A6
Monksbarn RG2 23 G2
Montague St, Caversham RG4 19 E1
Montague St, Reading RG1 19 F4
Montgomery Dr RG7 29 E5
Montpelier Dr RG4 11 G3
Moor Copse Cl RG6 24 B1
Moorhen Dr RG6 24 B2
Morecambe Av RG4 10 B3
Moreleigh Cl RG2 23 E5
Morgan Rd RG1 19 E5
Moriston Cl RG30 9 G6
Morlais RG4 10 C3
Morlands Av RG30 17 F4
Morpeth Cl RG2 23 F1
Mortimer Cl RG2 23 F6
Moss Cl RG4 11 E5
Mount Pleasant RG1 19 E5
Mount Pleasant Gro RG1 19 E5
Mount St, Collis St RG2 18 D5
Mount St, Essex St RG2 18 D5
Mowbray Dr RG30 9 F6
Muirfield Cl RG1 19 F4
Mulberry Cl RG5 21 E5

Mullens Ter RG4 10 A1
Mundesley St RG1 3 C4
Munro Av RG5 21 E6
Mustard La RG4 21 E1
Mylum Cl RG2 23 F6
Myrtle Cl RG31 8 B3

Nabbs Hill Cl RG31 16 B3
Napier Rd RG1 3 D1
Narrowmine Dr
  RG31 17 E5
Nash Cl RG6 24 A2
Neath Gdns RG30 17 E1
Nelson Rd RG4 11 E6
Netley Cl RG2 11 G2
Nevis Rd RG31 8 C3
New Bath Rd RG10 13 G4
New Bright St RG1 3 C4
New Hill RG8 8 B2
New Lane Hill RG30 16 D2
New Rd,
  Reading RG1 19 F6
New Rd,
  Sindlesham RG41 25 G5
New Rd,
  Sonning RG4 12 C4
Newark St RG1 3 D4
Newbery Cl RG31 8 C5
Newbury Cl RG10 13 H5
Newcastle Rd RG2 23 E1
Newlands Av RG4 10 D5
Newlyn Gdns RG2 23 E3
Newmarket Cl RG6 24 D3
Newport Rd RG1 18 C1
Newquay Dr RG6 24 B4
Newstead Rise RG2 23 G3
Newton Av RG4 11 G3
Nightingale Rd RG5 20 C6
Nimrod Cl RG5 21 G3
Nimrod Way RG2 18 D6
Nire Rd RG4 11 G6
Norcot Rd RG30 8 D6
Nores Rd RG2 23 F5
Norfolk Rd RG30 17 H1
Norman Pl RG1 3 D1
Norman Rd RG4 11 F5
Normanstead Rd
  RG31 8 B6
Norris Grn RG5 21 G1
Norris Rd RG6 20 A4
North Lodge Mews
  RG1 18 A6
North St,
  Caversham RG4 10 D6
North St,
  Reading RG1 3 A2
Northam Cl RG6 25 E2
Northbourne RG6 24 B3
Northbrook Rd RG4 11 F3
Northcourt Av RG2 19 F6
Northern Way RG2 22 C4
Northfield Cotts RG1 3 B1
Northfield Rd RG1 3 B1
Northumberland Av
  RG2 19 E6
Norton Rd,
  Reading RG1 19 G3
Norton Rd,
  Woodley RG5 21 F5
Norwich Dr RG5 20 C2
Norwood Rd RG1 19 G3
Notton Way RG6 23 H5
Nursery Gdns RG8 8 A1
Nuthatch Dr RG6 20 C6
Nutmeg Cl RG6 24 A3
Nutters La RG7 29 H6

Oak Dr RG5 21 G5
Oak Grn RG2 3 F5
Oak Tree Copse RG31 8 D4
Oak Tree Rd RG31 8 C5
Oak Tree Walk RG8 8 C1

Oak Vw RG31 8 C6
Oak Way RG5 20 D6
Oakdale Cl RG31 8 B6
Oakdale Walk RG5 21 G2
Oakham Cl RG31 8 C4
Oaklands RG1 19 H4
Oakley Rd RG4 10 C5
Oakside Way RG2 23 H4
Oatlands Rd RG2 29 H2
Oban Gdns RG5 21 E6
Odell Cl RG6 24 B4
Odiham Av RG4 11 G3
Ogmore Cl RG30 16 D1
Old Acre La RG10 13 H4
Old Barn Cl RG4 10 D2
Old Bath Rd,
  Calcot RG31 16 C4
Old Bath Rd,
  Charvil RG10 13 G5
Old Bath Rd,
  Sonning RG4 20 C1
Old Elm Dr RG30 16 C1
Old Farm Cres RG31 8 D5
Old Forest Rd RG41 26 C4
Old Whitley Wood La
  RG2 29 F1
Oldean Cl RG31 8 C6
Oldfield Cl RG4 20 B4
Oliver Dr RG31 16 B4
Onslow Gdns RG4 11 F5
Oracle Parkway RG6 20 A2
Orchard Cl,
  Purley-on-Thames
  RG31 8 B2
Orchard Cl,
  Spencers Wood
  RG7 29 E4
Orchard Ct RG2 23 F6
Orchard Gro RG4 11 G4
Orchard St RG1 3 C4
Oregon Av RG31 8 C3
Orkney Cl RG31 16 D5
Ormsby St RG1 18 B3
Orrin Cl RG30 17 F1
Orts Rd RG1 3 F3
Orville Cl RG5 21 G4
Orwell Cl RG4 10 B4
Osborne Rd RG30 9 G6
Osterley Ct RG1 19 G4
Osterley Dr RG4 11 G3
Overbury Av RG4 26 D4
Overdown Rd RG31 8 B5
Overlanders End
  RG31 9 E4
Owston Rd RG6 24 C3
Oxford Rd,
  Purley-on-Thames
  RG8,31 8 B1
Oxford Rd,
  Reading RG1 3 A3
Oxford Rd,
  Tilehurst RG30,31 9 E4
Oxford St RG4 10 D6

Paddick Cl RG4 13 E6
Paddick Dr RG6 24 D4
Paddock Rd RG4 19 F1
Padstow Gdns RG2 23 E3
Palmer Park Av RG6 20 A4
Palmera Av RG31 16 C5
Palmerstone Rd RG6 20 B4
Pangbourne St RG30 9 G6
Paprika Cl RG1 24 A3
Park Cres RG30 17 F2
Park Gro RG30 17 G2
Park La, Charvil RG10 13 G4
Park La,
  Tilehurst RG31 16 B2
Park View Dr North
  RG10 13 G3
Park View Dr South
  RG10 13 G4

Park Walk RG8 8 C1
Parkcorner La RG2 25 E6
Parkhill Dr RG31 4 F5
Parkhouse La RG30 18 A4
Parkside Rd RG30 17 H2
Parkway Dr RG4 13 E6
Parsley Cl RG6 23 H4
Parthia Cl RG1 3 C4
Partridge Dr RG31 16 B2
Pasture Cl RG6 24 B4
Patrick Rd RG4 19 E1
Patriot Pl RG1 3 F3
Pattinson Rd RG2 29 F1
Pavenham Cl RG6 24 B4
Pearmans Glade
  RG2 23 H4
Pearmans La RG6 23 H5
Pearmans La RG2 24 A5
Pearson Rd RG4 12 D5
Pearson Way RG5 21 E5
Peel Cl,
  Caversham RG4 11 F6
Peel Cl,
  Woodley RG5 21 H3
Pegasus Ct RG31 16 B1
Pegs Green Cl RG30 17 G2
Pelham St RG30 18 A4
Pell St RG1 18 D5
Pemberton Gdns
  RG31 16 C5
Pembroke Pl RG4 11 F5
Pendennis Av RG4 11 G2
Pendred Rd RG2 23 F6
Penn Cl RG4 10 D3
Pennine Cl RG31 16 A2
Pennine Way RG10 13 H4
Penny Royal Ct RG1 18 C5
Penroth Av RG30 17 H2
Penrose Av RG5 21 E4
Pentland Cl RG30 17 E4
Peppard Rd RG4 10 D6
Peppard Rd RG4 11 E1
Pepper La RG6 23 G1
Perimeter Rd RG5 21 G3
Perth Cl RG5 21 F1
Petworth Av RG30 17 F5
Petworth Ct RG1 18 B4
Pevensey Av RG4 11 G3
Pheasant La RG41 26 A3
Phillimore Rd RG4 11 E1
Phillips Cl RG5 21 H2
Phoebe Ct RG1 18 D4
Pickwell Cl RG6 24 C3
Picton Way RG4 10 D4
Piercefield RG31 16 B5
Pierces Hill RG31 8 B5
Piggotts Rd RG4 19 F1
Pikeshaw Way RG31 8 C5
Pimento Dr RG6 24 A3
Pincents La RG31 16 A3
Pinetree Ct RG4 10 D3
Pinewood Dr RG4 10 B3
Pingewood Rd South
  RG30 22 A6
Pitcroft Av RG6 20 A5
Pitford Rd RG5 21 F3
Pitts La RG6 20 B3
Players Grn RG5 21 E5
Playhatch Rd RG4 12 A4
Plumtrees RG6 24 B2
Plymouth Av RG4 20 C5
Plympton Cl RG6 25 E2
Pollards Way RG31 16 C4
Polsted Rd RG31 8 D6
Pond Head La RG6 20 D6
Poole Cl RG30 17 E2
Poplar Av RG30 17 E3
Poplar Gdns RG2 23 G3
Poplar La RG41 26 B1
Poppy Way RG31 16 B3
Porchfield Cl RG6 24 A3
Porlock Pl RG31 16 B5

Porter Cl RG6 24 C4
Portland Gdns RG30 16 C2
Portman Rd RG30 9 G6
Portmerion Gdns
  RG30 9 E5
Portrush Cl RG5 20 D4
Portway Cl RG1 18 B5
Post Horn Pl RG31 17 E4
Pottery Rd RG30 9 G6
Pound La RG4 12 D5
Preston Rd RG2 18 D6
Priest Hill RG4 10 C6
Primrose Cl RG8 8 C1
Primrose La RG41 26 A1
Prince Of Wales Av
  RG30 18 A3
Prince William Dr
  RG31 8 B5
Princes St RG1 3 F4
Priory Av RG4 10 D6
Priory Ct RG41 26 A2
Privet Cl RG6 24 B3
Promenade Rd RG4 18 D1
Prospect St,
  Caversham RG4 10 D6
Prospect St,
  Reading RG1 18 B4
Purley La RG8 8 B1
Purley Rise RG8 8 A1
Purley Village RG8 8 B1
Pursers Farm RG7 28 D4

Quantock Av RG4 11 G3
Quantock Cl RG10 13 H4
Queen Annes Gate
  RG4 11 E6
Queen St RG4 10 C5
Queen Victoria St RG1 3 D4
Queens Cotts RG1 3 E3
Queens Lawn RG1 19 G5
Queens Rd,
  Caversham RG4 19 E1
Queens Rd,
  Reading RG1 3 D3
Queens Walk RG1 3 B3
Queensborough Dr
  RG4 10 B3
Queensway RG4 11 F3
Quentin Rd RG5 20 D4

Radbourne Rd RG31 16 C5
Radcot Cl RG5 21 E2
Radnor Rd RG6 24 C1
Radstock La RG6 24 B2
Radstock Rd RG1 19 H3
Ragglewood Cl RG6 24 C1
Raglan Ct RG2 23 F3
Raglan Gdns RG4 11 E5
Ragley Mews RG4 11 G2
Railton Cl RG2 23 F6
Rainbow Pk RG41 25 H3
Rainworth Cl RG6 24 A5
Raleigh Cl RG5 21 E5
Ramsbury Dr RG6 24 A1
Randolph Rd RG1 18 C1
Rangewood Av RG30 17 E5
Ratby Cl RG6 24 C3
Ravenglass Cl RG6 24 C2
Ravensbourne Dr
  RG5 21 E2
Reading Bridge RG1 19 E2
Reading Rd,
  Winnersh RG41 25 F1
Reading Rd,
  Woodley RG5 20 C2
Reading Relief Rd
  RG2 22 C3
Recreation La RG7 28 D4
Recreation Rd RG30 8 D6
Rectory Rd RG4 10 D6
Red Cottage Dr
  RG31 16 B4

Red House Cl RG6 24 B
Redberry Cl RG4 11 G
Redhatch Dr RG6 24 A
Redlands Rd RG1 3 F
Redlane Ct RG1 19 F
Redruth Gdns RG2 23 E
Redwood Av RG5 21 G
Redwood Way RG31 8 C
Reeds Av RG6 24 A
Regency Heights
  RG4 10 B
Regent Cl RG6 24 C
Regent Ct RG1 3 E
Regent St RG1 19 C
Regis Cl RG2 23
Rembrandt Way RG1 18
Renault Rd RG5 21 G
Repton Rd RG6 24
Restwold Cl RG30 17
Retford Cl RG5 21
Reynards Cl RG41 26
Rhigos RG4 10
Rhine Cl RG4 11
Rhodes Cl RG6 25
Ribbleton Cl RG6 25
Richborough Cl RG6 24
Richfield Av RG1 18
Richmond Rd,
  Caversham RG4 10
Richmond Rd,
  Reading RG30 17
Rickman Cl RG5 20
Ridge Hall Cl RG4 10
Ridgemount Cl RG31 8
Ridlington Cl RG6 25
Righton Cl RG10 13
Riley Rd RG30
Ringwood Rd RG30
Ripley Rd RG30
Rissington Cl RG31
River Gdns RG8
River Rd,
  Caversham RG4 1
River Rd,
  Reading RG1
Riverdene Dr RG41
Rivermead Rd RG5
Riversdale Ct RG1
Riverside Ct RG4
Robin Hood La
  RG41
Robin Hood Way
  RG41
Robin Way RG31
Robindale Av RG6
Robinson Cl RG6
Rochester Av RG5
Rockbourne Gdns
  RG30
Rodney Cl RG1
Rodway Rd RG30
Rodwell Dr RG2
Roebuck Rise RG31
Rokeby Dr RG4
Roman Way RG6
Romany Cl RG30
Romany La RG30
Romsey Cl RG6
Romsey Rd RG30
Rona Ct RG30
Rose Cl RG5
Rose Kiln La RG1,2
Rose Walk RG1
Rosebery Rd RG4
Rosecroft Way RG2
Rosedale Cres RG6
Rosehill Pk RG4
Rosemary Av RG6
Rosemead Av RG31
Rosewood RG5
Roslyn Rd RG5
Ross Rd RG1

36

ossendale Rd RG4 11 F5
ossington Pl RG2 23 F4
otherfield Way RG4 10 D4
othwell Gdns RG5 21 F1
othwell Walk RG4 11 F6
oundabout La
 RG41 26 C4
outh La RG30 16 D2
ow La RG4 11 G1
owallan Cl RG4 11 F2
wan Dr RG5 21 E2
we Ct RG30 9 G6
wland Way RG6 23 H2
wley Rd RG2 19 E6
yal Av RG31 16 A4
yal Ct RG1 3 E3
yal Way RG2 22 C4
yston Ct RG1 17 E1
fus Issacs Rd RG4 11 E6
pert Sq RG1 19 G3
pert St RG1 19 G3
upert Walk,
 Avon RG1 19 G3
shall Cl RG6 23 H5
shbrook Rd RG5 20 D4
hden Dr RG2 23 G4
hey Way RG6 23 H4
hmoor Gdns
 G31 16 A5
sell Rd RG4 10 A1
sell St RG1 3 A4
sell Way RG41 25 H3
set Glade RG4 11 F1
tington Cl RG6 24 B4
erford Walk
 31 16 A2
and Rd RG30 17 H2
al Av RG30 9 E4
roft Cl RG5 21 E1
sh La RG7 29 E4
l Way RG6 23 H5
one Rd RG30 9 H6

ville St RG1 3 B2
ers Ct RG41 26 B4
ers Rd RG41 25 H5
ers La RG41 26 B4
on Cl RG6 24 C1
Cl RG6 24 A4
Rd RG31 8 B3
nes Mews RG2 23 E3
drews Ct RG1 19 G4
drews Rd RG4 10 C5
nes Rd RG4 10 C6
rnabas Rd,
 mer Green RG4 10 D3
rnabas Rd,
 ding RG2 23 H3

tholomews Rd
 19 H3
nus Rd RG31 16 C4
herines Cl
 1 25 G4
ilia Ct RG2 23 E2
ments Cl RG6 24 C4
ids Cl RG4 10 B4
vards Rd RG6 20 A4
abeth Ct RG2 23 E5
rges Rd RG30 9 G6
rges Ter RG30 9 G6
s Cl RG1 3 D4
ns Cl RG5 21 F2
ns Hill RG1 3 F3
ns Rd,
 rsham RG4 11 E6
s Rd,
 ng RG1 3 F4
s RG1 3 F3
s Way RG4 11 E4
ns Cl RG6 24 C3
s Av RG8 8 C1

St Marys Butts RG1 3 C3
St Marys Rd RG41 25 G4
St Michaels Rd RG30 16 C1
St Patricks Av RG10 13 G3
St Pauls Ct RG1 18 D5
St Peters Av RG4 10 A4
St Peters Hill RG4 10 C5
St Peters Rd RG6 20 A5
St Ronans Rd RG30 17 G1
St Saviours Rd RG1 18 B5
St Saviours Ter RG1 18 C5
St Stephens Cl RG4 18 D1
Salcombe Dr RG6 20 B6
Salcombe Rd RG6 23 F1
Saleby Cl RG6 25 E2
Salford Cl RG2 23 E5
Salisbury Rd RG30 18 B2
Salmon Cl RG7 29 E5
Salmond Rd RG2 23 F6
Saltersgate Cl RG6 24 D3
Sampage Cl RG2 23 E6
Sanctuary RG30 9 E6
Sandcroft Rd RG4 10 B3
Sandford Dr RG5 21 F1
Sandford La RG5 21 H3
Sandford Rd RG30 9 E4
*Sandhills Way,
 Millers Gro RG31 17 E4
Sandleford Cl RG2 23 E6
Sandown Ar RG31 16 B4
Sandringham Way
 RG31 16 A4
Sandstone Cl RG41 26 A4
Sarum Ct RG30 18 A4
Saunders Ct RG8 8 B2
Savernake Cl RG30 17 E1
Sawtry Cl RG6 25 E2
Scafell Cl RG31 8 B5
Scholars Cl RG4 10 C6
School Grn RG2 29 H3
School La,
 Caversham RG4 10 D6
School La,
 Emmer Green RG4 11 E3
School Rd RG31 8 C6
School Ter RG1 19 G3
Scott Cl,
 Emmer Green RG4 10 D4
Scott Cl,
 Woodley RG5 21 G3
Scours La RG30 9 G5
Seaford Gdns RG5 21 E5
Seaton Gdns RG2 23 F2
Selborne Ct RG1 3 E3
Selborne Gdns RG30 9 F5
Selcourt Cl RG5 20 D2
Sellafield Way RG6 24 C2
Selsdon Av RG5 21 F2
Selsey Way RG6 24 B4
Send Rd RG4 19 F1
Seton Dr RG31 17 E4
Sevenoaks Dr RG7 28 D4
Sevenoaks Rd RG6 24 B1
Severn Way RG30 17 E2
Sewell Av RG41 26 E4
Seymour Av RG2 29 H1
Shaftesbury Rd RG30 9 G6
Shakespeare Cl RG4 11 G3
Shakleton Way RG5 21 G3
Sharnwood Dr RG31 17 E4
Sharpethorpe Cl
 RG6 24 B4
Shaw Rd RG1 18 C5
Sheep Walk RG4 10 D4
Sheldon Gdns RG2 23 E4
Shelgate Walk RG5 20 C4
Shelley Cl RG5 21 E6
Shenstone Rd RG2 19 E6
Shepherds Av RG6 20 B2
Shepherds Hill RG6 20 B2
Shepherds House La
 RG6 20 A2

Shepherds La RG4 10 A3
Shepherds Walk RG6 20 C2
Shepley Dr RG30 17 H4
Sheraton Dr RG31 8 B6
Sherbourne Dr RG5 21 F3
Sherfield Cl RG2 23 F1
Sherfield Dr RG2 23 F1
Sheridan Av RG4 10 C4
Sherman Pl RG1 18 D4
Sherman Rd RG1 18 D4
Sherwood Pl RG8 8 B2
Sherwood Rd RG41 26 A2
Sherwood Rise RG8 8 A2
Sherwood St RG30 9 H6
Shinfield Rd RG2 19 F6
Shinfield Rise RG2 23 H3
Shipley Cl RG5 21 G1
Shipton Cl RG31 8 B4
Shireshead Cl RG30 17 H2
Shirley Av RG2 23 F6
Shooters Way RG2 22 C4
Short St,
 Caversham RG4 10 D6
Short St,
 Reading RG1 19 E5
Shrubland Dr RG30 17 F5
Sibley Park Rd RG4 24 A3
Sibson RG6 24 C2
Sidmouth Grange Cl
 RG6 20 B3
Sidmouth Grange Rd
 RG6 20 B3
Sidmouth St RG1 3 E3
Silbury Cl RG31 16 A5
Silcester Rd RG30 17 H4
Silver Fox Cres RG5 20 D4
Silver St RG1 3 D4
Silverdale Rd RG6 24 B1
Silverthorne Dr RG4 10 A3
Simmonds St RG1 3 C3
Simmons Fields
 RG10 13 H5
Simons Cl RG31 8 B2
Simons La RG41 26 C4
Sindle Cl RG41 25 H3
Skeffling Cl RG6 25 E3
Skelmerdale Way
 RG6 25 E1
Skerritt Way RG8 8 C2
Skilton Rd RG31 8 B4
Skye Cl RG31 16 D5
Small Mead Rd RG2 22 A4
Smallmead Rd RG2 22 C3
Snowden Dr RG31 16 A2
Snowdrop Gro RG41 26 A2
Soane End RG4 10 C2
Soham Cl RG6 24 C4
Solent Ct RG1 3 C4
Somerset Walk RG31 16 A2
Somerstown Ct RG1 18 B4
Somerton Gdns RG6 24 B3
Sonning La RG4 12 D6
Sonning Mdws RG4 20 C1
Sopwith Cl RG5 21 G4
South Dr, Earley RG2 23 H3
South Dr,
 Sonning RG4 20 C1
South Glade RG2 23 F5
South Lake Cres RG5 21 E5
South Oak Way RG2 22 B5
South St,
 Caversham RG4 10 D6
South St,
 Reading RG1 3 D4
South View Av RG4 11 E6
South View Pk RG4 11 E6
Southampton St RG1 3 C4
Southcote Farm La
 RG30 17 H4
Southcote La RG30 17 H4
Southcote Rd RG30 18 A5
Southdown Rd RG4 10 D4

Southern Ct RG1 3 D4
Southern Hill RG1 19 F5
Southerndene Cl
 RG31 8 C5
Southwold Cl RG6 24 D3
Sovereign Way RG31 16 B4
Spencer Rd RG2 23 E5
Spenwood Cl RG7 28 D5
Spey Rd RG30 17 F1
Spinney Cl RG4 11 F1
Spitfire Way RG5 21 G3
Spode Cl RG30 9 E6
Spring Gdns RG7 28 D5
Spring Gro RG1 19 E5
Spring La RG4 12 B2
Spring Ter RG2 19 E5
Springdale RG6 24 B3
Springfield Mews
 RG4 11 E4
Spruce Rd RG5 21 G5
Squirrels Way RG6 24 B3
Staddlestone Cl RG31 8 B4
Stadium Way RG30 9 G5
Stafford Cl RG5 21 F3
Staffordshire Cl RG30 9 E6
Stanbury Gate RG2 28 D4
Stanham Rd RG30 17 E1
Stanhope Rd RG2 23 F1
Stanley Gro RG1 18 B3
Stanley St RG1 3 A2
Stanshawe Rd RG1 3 B2
Stanton Cl RG6 20 C6
Stapleford Rd RG30 17 H4
Star La RG1 3 D3
Star Rd RG4 11 F6
Starlings Dr RG31 16 B3
Station App RG1 3 C2
Station Hill RG1 3 C2
Station Rd,
 Earley RG6 20 C6
Station Rd,
 Reading RG1 3 C2
Staverton Rd RG2 23 F1
Steeple Walk RG6 23 H4
Steggles Cl RG5 20 D2
Sterling Way RG30 9 G6
*Stettrington Cl,
 Easington Dr RG6 25 E3
Stilton Cl RG6 25 E2
Stirling Cl RG4 11 G3
Stockbury Cl RG6 24 B3
Stockton Rd RG2 23 E4
Stone St RG30 9 G5
Stonea Cl RG6 24 C4
Stoneham Cl RG30 17 F2
Stonehaven Dr RG5 21 G4
Stour Cl RG30 17 F1
Stowmarket Cl RG6 24 D3
Strand Way RG6 24 C4
Stratford Way RG2 16 A2
Stratheden Pl RG1 3 A2
Strathmore Dr RG10 13 G4
Strathy Cl RG30 9 G6
Stratton Gdns RG2 23 E4
Stuart Cl RG4 10 D3
Studland Cl RG2 23 E5
Sturbridge Cl RG6 24 C3
Suffolk Rd RG30 17 H2
Sulham Walk RG30 17 H4
Summerfield Cl
 RG41 26 E3
Sun St RG1 19 G3
Sunderland Cl RG5 21 H3
Sundial Ct RG30 17 F2
Surley Row RG4 10 D3
Surrey Rd RG2 23 E1
Sussex Gdns RG5 21 E4
Sussex La RG7 29 F5
Sutcliffe Av RG6 24 D3
Sutherland Gro RG31 16 D5
Sutherlands Av RG2 19 F5
Sutton Ct RG6 20 B4

Sutton Walk RG1 19 F5
Suttons Park Av RG6 19 H2
Swainstone Rd RG2 19 E6
Swallow Cl RG31 8 B1
Swallowfield Dr RG2 23 E6
Swan Pl RG1 3 C4
Swanholm Gdns
 RG31 17 E4
Swanmore Cl RG6 25 E3
Swansea Rd RG1 3 B1
Swansea Ter RG31 8 D5
Sweet Briar Dr RG31 16 B5
Swepstone Cl RG6 24 C3
Swinbrook Cl RG31 8 C3
Swiss Cottage Cl
 RG31 8 B6
Sycamore Cl RG5 20 C6
Sycamore Rd RG2 23 G2
Sylvan Walk RG30 17 H4
Sylvester Cl RG41 26 B1

Tadcroft Walk RG31 16 D5
Taff Way RG30 17 F2
Tagg La RG4 12 A1
Talbot Cl RG4 11 F6
Talbot Ct RG1 3 B4
Talbot Way RG31 8 B3
Talfourd Av RG6 20 A6
Tallis La RG30 17 H4
Tamar Gdns RG2 23 F2
Tamarind Way RG6 23 H3
Tamarisk Av RG2 23 G3
Tamworth Cl RG6 24 C3
Tanners La RG4 10 C1
Targett Ct RG41 25 H3
Tarlton Cl RG30 17 E2
Tarragon Cl RG6 23 H3
Tavistock Rd RG2 23 E2
Tay Rd RG30 17 F1
Taylor Ct RG1 18 B4
Taynton Walk RG2 19 E5
Tazewell Ct RG1 18 B4
Telford Cres RG5 21 F2
Temple Mews RG5 21 F4
Temple Pl RG1 3 C4
Templeton Gdns
 RG2 23 E3
Tenby Av RG4 11 G3
Tennyson Rd RG5 21 E6
Tern Cl RG30 17 F2
Tessa Rd RG1 18 C1
Test Cl RG30 17 F1
Tetbury Ct RG1 18 B4
Teviot Rd RG30 16 D1
Thames Av RG1 18 D1
Thames Dr RG10 13 F2
Thames Reach RG8 8 C2
Thames Side RG1 18 D1
Thames Side Prom
 RG1 3 D1
Thames St RG4 12 D5
Thames Ter RG4 12 D5
Thames Valley Park Dr
 RG6 19 H2
Thanington Way RG6 24 B3
The Bader Way RG5 21 F6
The Beeches RG31 8 D3
The Birchwoods
 RG31 16 A1
The Brookmill RG1 18 B6
The Causeway RG4 19 F1
The Cedars RG31 8 C5
The Chancellors Way
 RG2 19 G6
The Chase RG31 16 C5
The Cloisters RG4 10 C6
The Close RG5 21 E5
The Crescent RG6 24 C1
The Crest RG4 11 E3
The Dell RG1 3 E4
The Delph RG6 24 D2
The Drive RG6 20 A3

The Fells RG31 16 A2
The Firs RG1 3 A4
The Forbury RG1 3 D2
The Glade RG8 8 B2
The Grange RG4 10 A2
The Grove RG1 3 E4
The Hawthorns RG10 13 G5
The Holt RG8 8 C2
The Horse Cl RG4 11 E4
The Hydes RG31 8 B3
The Knapp RG6 20 B6
The Knoll RG31 8 A5
The Lawns RG2 23 F2
The Manor RG2 29 G2
The Maying RG2 23 E6
The Meadway RG30 16 C2
The Mews RG1 19 H4
The Mount, Caversham RG4 10 C6
The Mount, Reading RG1 19 F5
The Old La RG1 18 B6
The Old Orchard RG31 16 D4
The Parade, Brecon Rd, Woodley RG5 21 F2
The Parade, Coppice Rd, Woodley RG5 21 E6
The Parade, Southcote RG30 17 H4
The Priory RG4 26 A2
The Queens Dr RG2 19 G6
The Ridgeway, Caversham RG4 10 D5
The Ridgeway, Woodley RG5 21 E6
The Ridings RG4 11 E1
The Rise RG4 11 E4
The Sadlers RG31 8 B5
The Short RG8 8 C1
The Slopes RG4 11 F6
The Spinney RG31 16 D4
The Square, Earley RG6 24 A4
The Square, Spencers Wood RG7 28 D5
The Triangle RG30 16 C1
The Warren RG4 9 H3
The Willows RG4 18 D1
Theobald Dr RG31 8 C3
Thetford Mews RG4 11 G3
Thicket Rd RG30 9 E1
Thirlmere Av RG30 9 E4
Thistledown RG31 8 B5
Thistleton Way RG6 25 E2
Thomson Walk RG31 16 D4
Thorn La RG1 3 D3
Thorn St RG1 3 B3
Thornbers Way RG10 13 H4
Thornbridge Rd RG2 23 E5
Thorney Cl RG6 25 E2
Thornton Mews RG30 9 H6
Thornton Rd RG30 9 H6
Thrale Mews RG30 17 G1
Thurlestone Gdns RG2 23 E2
Thurnscoe Cl RG6 23 H5
Thurso Cl RG30 9 F6
Thyme Cl RG6 24 A4
Tickhill Cl RG6 23 H5
Tidmarsh St RG30 9 G6
Tiger Cl RG6 21 G3
Tilbury Cl RG4 11 F5
Tilehurst Rd RG1,30 3 A4
Tilling RG31 8 A5
Tilney Way RG6 24 A5
Tinsley Cl RG6 24 A5
Tintern Cres RG1 18 B6
Tinwell Cl RG6 25 E2
Tippet Rise RG2 18 D5

Tippings La RG5 21 F2
Tiptree Cl RG6 23 H4
Tithebarn Gro RG31 17 E4
Tiverton Cl RG6 23 H1
Tofrek Ter RG30 17 H1
Tokersgreen Rd RG4 10 A2
Torcross Gro RG31 16 B5
Torrington Rd RG2 23 F3
Toseland Way RG6 25 E2
Totnes Rd RG2 23 F3
Toutley Cl RG41 26 D4
Toutley Rd RG41 26 E3
Tower Cl RG4 11 E1
Town Pl RG1 3 F3
Trafalgar Ct RG30 18 A5
Trafford Rd RG1 10 C3
Tredegar Rd RG4 10 C3
Tree Cl RG30 16 C1
Treeton Cl RG6 23 H5
Treforgan RG4 10 C3
Trelawney Dr RG31 8 B5
Trelleck Rd RG1 18 C6
Trenthams Cl RG8 8 B2
Treyarnon Ct RG1 19 H4
Tring Rd RG31 8 C4
Trinity Pl RG1 3 A3
Triumph Cl RG5 21 F6
Troon Ct RG1 19 F4
Trout Cl RG6 20 A2
Trusthorpe Cl RG6 25 E2
Tudor Rd RG1 3 B2
Tuns Hill Cotts RG6 20 A6
Tupsley Rd RG1 18 B6
Turmeric Cl RG6 24 A3
Turnbridge Cl RG6 24 B4
Turnstone Cl RG41 25 G2
Tuscan Cl RG30 8 D6
Tuxford Mews RG30 17 G2
Tweed Ct RG1 17 G1
Twin Oaks RG4 11 E2
Twyford Rd RG40 26 F2
Tyberton Pl RG1 18 C6
Tyle Rd RG30 16 C1
Tyler Cl RG4 10 B3
Tylers Pl RG30 9 E6
Tylorstown RG4 10 C3

Uffcott Cl RG6 23 H5
Uffington Cl RG31 16 B1
Ullswater Dr RG31 8 C3
Ulster Cl RG3 11 G3
Underwood Rd RG30 17 E4
Union St RG1 3 C2
Unity Cl RG4 11 E3
Unity Ct RG4 11 E3
Upavon Dr RG4 18 B5
Uplands Rd RG4 10 B3
Upper Crown St RG1 19 E4
Upper Meadow Rd RG2 23 F2
Upper Redlands Rd RG1 19 H5
Upper Warren Av RG4 9 H3
Upper Woodcote Rd RG4 10 A3
Uppingham Dr RG5 21 F1
Uppingham Gdns RG4 11 G2
Upton Rd RG30 17 F2
Usk Rd RG30 17 E2

Vachel Rd RG1 3 B2
Vale Cres RG30 9 E5
Vale Vw RG10 13 H5
Valentia Cl RG30 18 A2
Valentia Rd RG30 18 A3
Valentine Cl RG2 23 H4
Valentine Cres RG4 11 F5
Valerie Ct RG1 18 B5
Valley Cl RG4 10 B3
Valpy St RG1 3 D2
Vanbrugh Ct RG1 19 G4

Vanlore Way RG31 16 B4
Vastern Rd RG1 3 C1
Vauxhall Dr RG5 21 F4
Venetia Cl RG4 11 F1
Ventnor Rd RG31 8 C6
Verbena Cl RG41 25 G1
Verney Mews RG30 17 G2
Vernon Cres RG2 23 E6
Vicarage Rd RG2 19 F6
Vicarage Wood Way RG31 8 A5
Vickers Cl, Shinfield RG2 29 H2
Vickers Cl, Woodley RG5 21 G4
Victor Way RG5 21 G3
Victoria Mews RG30 17 H2
Victoria Rd, Caversham RG4 10 C5
Victoria Rd, Tilehurst RG31 8 C6
Victoria Sq RG1 19 F3
Victoria St RG1 19 F4
Victoria Way RG1 19 G3
Village Cl RG2 23 E6
Vincent Cl RG5 21 F4
Vine Cres RG30 17 F5
Virginia Way RG30 17 G4
Viscount Way RG5 21 F4
Voller Dr RG31 16 B3
Vulcan Cl RG5 21 H2

Waingels Rd RG10 13 G6
Waldeck St RG2 18 D5
Walkers Pl RG30 17 H1
Wallace Cl RG5 20 D5
Waller Ct RG4 11 E6
Walmer Rd RG30 17 F3
Walmer Rd RG5 21 F1
Walnut Way RG30 16 C1
Walrus Cl RG5 21 H3
Walton Cl RG5 20 C3
Wandhope Way RG31 8 B4
Wantage Rd RG30 17 H2
Warbler Cl RG31 16 B2
Warbler Dr RG6 24 B3
Warborough Av RG31 16 A1
Warbreck Dr RG31 16 A3
Wardle Av RG31 8 C5
Waring Cl RG6 24 C4
Warley Rise RG31 8 B3
Warnford Rd RG30 17 E1
Warnsham Cl RG6 24 B4
Warren Cl RG4 10 C6
Warren Rd RG4 20 D1
Warwick Rd RG2 19 E6
Washington Rd RG4 11 E6
Water Rd RG30 17 G1
Waterloo Rd RG2 18 D6
Waterloo Rise RG2 19 E6
Waterman Pl RG1 3 C1
Watersfield Cl RG6 24 B4
Waterside Dr RG8 8 C2
Waterside Gdns RG1 3 E3
Watlington St RG1 3 E3
Watmore La RG41 26 B2
Wavell Ct RG2 23 H4
Waverley Rd RG30 17 G1
Waybrook Cres RG1 19 H5
Waylen St RG1 3 A3
Weald Rise RG30 9 E5
Wealden Way RG30 8 D6
Weardale Cl RG4 10 C6
Wedderburn Cl RG41 26 B3
Wedgwood Way RG30 9 E6
Weighbridge Row RG1 3 A1
Weir Cl RG31 17 E4
Weirside Ct RG1 19 F3
Welby Cres RG41 25 H3
Willow Gdns,

Weldale Pl RG1 3 B2
Weldale St RG1 3 A2
Welford Rd RG5 21 G3
Welland Cl RG31 8 B6
Wellfield RG31 16 B1
Wellington Av RG2 23 G1
Wellington Ct RG7 28 C4
Welwick Cl RG6 25 E3
Wendover Way RG30 16 C1
Wenlock Edge RG10 13 G4
Wensley Rd RG1 18 A6
Wentworth Av RG2 23 F5
Wesley Gate RG1 3 E3
West Ct RG5 21 E1
West Dr, Clacot RG31 16 D4
West Dr, Sonning RG4 20 D1
West Fryerne RG30 17 H2
West Hill RG1 18 D5
West St RG1 3 B2
Westbourne Ter RG30 17 H1
Westbrook Rd RG30 9 H6
Westbury La RG8 8 A1
Westcote Rd RG30 18 A4
Westdene Cres RG4 10 A4
*Westerham Walk, Charndon RG2 19 E5
Western Av RG5 20 D3
Western Elms Av RG30 18 A4
Western Oaks RG31 8 D4
Western Rd RG1 18 B4
Westfield Rd, Caversham RG4 10 D6
Westfield Rd, Winnersh RG41 25 H3
Westlands Av RG2 23 H3
Westminster Way RG6 24 C3
Westonbirt Dr RG4 10 B5
Westridge Av RG8 8 B1
Westwood Glen RG31 8 B6
Westwood Rd RG31 8 C5
Westwood Row RG31 8 C4
Wetherby Cl RG4 11 E2
Wharfedale Rd RG41 25 F1
Wheatfields Rd RG2 29 H1
Wheatlands Cl RG31 17 E4
Wheatley Cl RG2 23 G4
Wheble Dr RG5 20 D3
Wheeler Ct RG31 8 D5
Wheelton Cl RG6 25 E1
Whitby Dr RG1 19 F5
Whitby Grn RG4 11 G3
White Lodge Cl RG31 8 A3
Whitegates La RG6 20 B3
Whiteknights Rd RG6 19 H5
Whitely St RG2 19 E5
Whitestone Cl RG6 25 E2
Whitley Park La RG2 19 F6
Whitley Wood La RG2 23 E5
Whitley Wood Rd RG2 23 E6
Whitstone Gdns RG2 23 E3
Whitton Cl RG6 24 D3
Wickford Way RG4 24 A4
Wickham Rd RG6 25 E3
Wickhambrook Cl RG6 24 D2
Widecombe Pl RG2 23 E3
Wield Ct RG6 25 E3
Wigmore La RG30 9 G5
Wild Cl RG6 24 C4
Wilderness Ct RG6 24 A1
Wilderness Rd RG6 20 A6
William St RG1 3 A2
Willow Gdns,

Reading RG2 23 G
Willow Gdns, Tilehurst RG31 8 A
Willow Ridge RG5 21 F
Willow Tree Glade RG31 16 B
Willowside RG5 21 F
Wilmington Cl RG5 21 F
Wilsford Cl RG6 23 F
Wilson Ct RG41 25 F
Wilson Rd RG30 17 F
Wilton Rd RG30 17 F
Wiltshire Walk RG31 16
Wilwyne Cl RG4 11
Wimblington Dr RG6 24
Wimborne Gdns RG30 9
Wincanton Rd RG2 23
Winchester Rd RG2 23
Wincroft Rd RG4 10
Windermere Cl RG41 26
Windermere Rd RG2 23
Windrush Ct RG30 17
Windrush Way RG30 17
Windsor Cl RG31 16
Windsor Sq RG1 19
Wingate Rd RG5 21
Wingrove Rd RG30 17
Winnersh Gate RG41 26
Winnersh Gro RG41 26
Winser Dr RG30 18
Winston Ct RG7 2
Winston Way RG30 1
Winterberry Way RG41 1
Winton Rd RG2 23
Wintringham Way RG8
Wispington Cl RG6 2
Wiston Ter RG1
Witcham Cl RG6 2
Withy Cl RG31 1
Wittenham Av RG31 1
Woburn Cl RG4 1
Wokingham Rd, Reading RG6 1
Wokingham Rd, Winnersh RG10 1
Wolseley St RG1
Wolsey Rd RG4
Wood Green RG2
Wood Green Cl RG30
Woodberry Cl RG4
Woodbine Cl RG6
Woodbridge Rd RG31
Woodcock Ct RG7
Woodcock La RG7
Woodcote Rd RG4
Woodcote Way RG4
Woodford Cl RG4
Woodhurst La RG41
Woodland Dr RG30
Woodlands Av, Winnersh RG41
Woodlands Av, Woodley RG5
Woodlands Gro RG4
Woodley Grn RG5
Woodman Cl RG2
Woodmere Cl RG6
Woodrow Ct RG4
Woods Rd RG4
Woodsend Cl RG6
Woodside Way RG2
Woodstock St RG1
Woodward Cl RG41
Woodwaye RG5
Woodyer Cl RG5
Woolacombe Dr RG6
Wootton Cl RG31
Worcester Cl RG30
Wordsworth Ct RG4

'orrall Way RG6 23 H5
'orton Dr RG2 22 D5
'orton Rd RG2 22 D5
'renfield Dr RG4 10 C4
'renswood Cl RG2 23 E6
'right Cl RG5 21 G4
'roxham Rd RG5 20 D2
ychcotes RG4 10 B6
ychelm Rd RG2 29 H2
ychwood Cl RG6 24 A2
ychwood Cres
RG6 24 A2
ye Cl RG30 17 E2
ykeham Rd RG6 20 A4
yncote RG2 23 H3
yndham Cres RG5 20 D2
ynford Cl RG30 17 G5
yre Ct RG31 8 B3
rnton Cl RG4 11 E2
verton Rd RG2 23 E2
v La RG1 18 B6
v Tree Rise RG31 16 B3
ld Hall Pl RG1 3 D3
eham Cl RG6 25 E3
k Rd RG1 3 B1
zan St RG1 3 A3

SONNING COMMON

letree Cl RG4 5 B3
ford Av RG4 5 B4
cerville Rd RG4 5 B4
ch Rise RG4 5 B3
n Cl RG4 5 C5
Wood Ct RG4 5 D5
kmore La RG4 5 D4
nts Court Rd RG9 5 C3
ley Cres RG4 5 A1
ds Cl RG4 5 C4
rs Orch RG4 5 A6
ng Rd RG4 5 B3
khouse Green Rd
'4 5 A6
ton Pl RG4 5 C5
ern Rd RG9 5 A1
ch La RG9 5 C1
hill Cres RG4 5 C3
rs La RG9 5 B1
ore La RG9 5 A1
ers Pightle RG4 5 A6
leaze RG4 5 A6
sley Way RG4 5 B4
a RG9 5 C1
La RG9 5 A1
La RG9 5 C1
t RG4 5 C5
Way RG4 5 D6
Carling La RG9 5 A1
ystree Rd RG9 5 A3
e Av RG9 5 D1
Hill RG9 5 C3
Hill Cres RG9 5 B3
La RG4 5 B4
Rd RG4 5 C5

Hazel Gdns RG4 5 C4
Hazelmoor La RG4 5 A5
Heather Cl RG4 5 C4
Hillcrest La RG9 5 C2
Horsepond Rd RG4 5 A3

Ilex Cl RG4 5 C5
Ilsley Cl RG4 5 B4
Inglewood Cl RG4 5 C4

Josey Cl RG4 5 C3

Kennylands Rd RG4 5 B5
Kidmore La RG4 5 A6

Lambourne Rd RG4 5 B4
Lea Rd RG4 5 C5

Maple Cl RG4 5 C5

Naish Way RG4 5 D6
Newfield Rd RG4 5 B3

Old Copse Gdns RG4 5 B3
Orchard Av RG4 5 B4

Pages Orch RG4 5 B4
Park Cl RG4 5 C3
Peppard Hill RG9 5 B2
Peppard Rd RG4 5 C3
Pond End Rd RG4 5 C3
Priory Copse RG9 5 C3

Reades La RG4 5 A4
Redhouse Dr RG4 5 C4
Rowan Cl RG4 5 C5
Russett Cl RG4 5 B4

Sedgefield Cl RG4 5 B3
Sedgewell Rd RG4 5 C4
Smith Cl RG4 5 B4
Springwood La RG9 5 C1
Stevens La RG9 5 A1
Stoke Row RG9 5 A1

Walnut Cl RG4 5 B4
Westleigh Dr RG4 5 C5
Widmore La RG4 5 C4
Wood La Cl RG4 5 C4
Wood La,
  Kidmore End RG4 5 A6
Wood La,
  Sonning Common
  RG4 5 B5
Woodlands Rd RG4 5 B3
Wychwood Cl RG4 5 B4
Wyfold La RG9 5 A1

THEALE

Alderfield Cl RG7 27 C1
Andrews Cl RG7 27 B2
Arrowhead Rd RG7 27 C3
Bath Rd RG7 27 A3
Blatchs Cl RG7 27 B2
Blossom Av RG7 27 B1
Blossom La RG7 27 C1
Brunel Rd RG7 27 B2
Cavalier Cl RG7 27 B2
Chestnut Cl RG7 27 C1
Church St RG7 27 B2

Cloister Mews RG7 27 B2
Crown La RG7 27 C2
Deadmans La RG7 27 A1
Elizabeth Ct RG7 27 C2
Ellerton Pl RG7 27 C1
Ely Rd RG7 27 C2
Englefield Rd RG7 27 A1
Exeter Way RG7 27 C2
High St RG7 27 C2

INDUSTRIAL & RETAIL:
Arlington Business Pk
  RG7 27 D2
Pincents Kiln
  Industrial Est RG7 27 D1
The Markham
  Centre Trading Est
  RG7 27 C3
Theale Commercial Est
  RG7 27 D2

James Butcher Dr
  RG7 27 C2
Kathleen Sanders Ct
  RG7 27 B1
Lambfields RG7 27 B2
Meadow Way RG7 27 B2
Morton Pl RG7 27 C1
Mulberry Way RG7 27 B2
Muswell Cl RG7 27 B2
Myton Walk RG7 27 B2
North St RG7 27 A1
North Walk RG7 27 B1
Nunhide La RG8 27 D1
Pangbourne Rd RG7 27 A1
Pincents La RG31 27 D1
Play Platt RG7 27 B1
Rotherfield Cl RG7 27 C1
Roundhead Rd RG7 27 B2
St Ives Cl RG7 27 B2
Station Rd RG7 27 C2
Swallowfield Gdns
  RG7 27 C1
The Courtyard RG7 27 B1
The Crescent RG7 27 B1
The Green RG7 27 A3
The Orchard RG7 27 C1
Trafalgar Ct RG7 27 B1
Trinity Ct RG7 27 B2
Volunteer Rd RG7 27 B2
Waterside Dr RG7 27 D2
Whitehart Cl RG7 27 C1
Wigmore La RG7 27 A3
Woodfield Way RG7 27 C2
Worsley Pl RG7 27 C1

TWYFORD

Amberley Dr RG10 14 A2
Arnside Cl RG10 14 B2

Badger Dr RG10 14 B1
Bell Ct RG10 14 A4
Bolwell Cl RG10 14 C5
Bridge Farm La RG10 14 A2
Broad Hinton RG10 14 C5
Broadwater Rd RG10 14 C6
Brook St RG10 14 B4
Burton Cl RG10 14 C6
Byron Cl RG10 14 B4
Byron Rd RG10 14 B5

Carlile Gdns RG10 14 A2
Castle End Rd RG10 14 D3
Chapel Row RG10 14 B4
Chaseside Av RG10 14 B2
Cheriton Av RG10 14 B2
Church La RG10 14 D3
Church St RG10 14 B4
Coleridge Cl RG10 14 C6
Colleton Dr RG10 14 B2
Cotterell Gdns RG10 14 C5
Crest Cl RG10 14 B2

Firgrove RG10 14 B1
Gas La RG10 14 B4
Gooch Cl RG10 14 C5
Harrison Cl RG10 14 D5
Hermitage Dr RG10 14 B4
Heron Dr RG10 14 B2
High St RG10 14 A4
Hilltop RG10 14 B4
Hogmoor La RG10 14 C6
Hubbard Cl RG10 14 C6
Hurst Pk Rd RG10 14 C6
Hurst Rd RG10 14 B4

INDUSTRIAL & RETAIL:
*Twyford Business Pk,
  Station Rd RG10 14 B4
Ruscombe Pk
  Industrial Est RG10 14 C3

Jarvis Dr RG10 14 B2
Kibblewhite Cres
  RG10 14 B2
Kingfisher Ct RG10 14 C5
Lincoln Gdns RG10 14 B3
Llewellyn Pk RG10 14 A2
Loddon Hall Rd RG10 14 B3
Loddon Vw RG10 14 B5
London Rd RG10 14 B4
Longfield Rd RG10 14 A3
Mallard Cl RG10 14 C5
Malvern Way RG10 14 B1
Maple Bank RG10 14 B2
Middlefields RG10 14 C2
Milton Way RG10 14 C3
New Bath Rd RG10 14 A2
New Rd,
  Ruscombe RG10 14 C2
New Rd,
  Twyford RG10 14 A2
Northbury Av RG10 14 C3
Northbury La RG10 14 C3
Old Bath Rd RG10 14 A4
Old Bath Rd RG10 14 C3
Old Mill Ct RG10 14 B4

Orchard Est RG10 14 C3
Packham Dr RG10 14 B2
Paddock Heights
  RG10 14 B5
Pennfields RG10 14 B2
Pine Gro RG10 14 B3
Polehampton Cl
  RG10 14 B4
Polehampton Ct
  RG10 14 B4
Poundfield Way
  RG10 14 C6
Royal Station Ct
  RG10 14 B4
Ruscombe La RG10 14 C3
Ruscombe Pk RG10 14 C3
Ruscombe Rd RG10 14 B3
St James Cl RG10 14 C3
St Michaels Ct RG10 14 B2
St Swithins RG10 14 B4
Saunders RG10 14 C6
Southbury La RG10 14 D3
Southview Cl RG10 14 B2
Springfield Pk RG10 14 B3
Stanlake La RG10 14 C5
Station Rd RG10 14 B4
Stephen Cl RG10 14 C6
Swans Ct RG10 14 B4
Sycamore Dr RG10 14 B3
The Grove RG10 14 B4
The Pines RG10 14 B1
Thornbury Grn RG10 14 B3
Treacher Ct RG10 14 C3
Troutbeck Cl RG10 14 B2
Verey Cl RG10 14 C5
Wagtail Cl RG10 14 B4
Walnut Tree Cl RG10 14 C2
Waltham Rd RG10 14 A1
Wargrave Rd RG10 14 A1
Weavers Way RG10 14 A4
Wensley Cl RG10 14 B4
Wessex Gdns RG10 14 C5
Westview Dr RG10 14 B2
Willow Dr RG10 14 B2
Winchcombe Rd
  RG10 14 B5
Woodpecker Cl RG10 14 C5
Yewhurst Cl RG10 14 A2

**For an up-to-date publication list and latest prices
visit our web site at**

www.estate-publications.co.uk

**Use the search facility to find the
village, town or city you require.**